Your Choice

Rodney Stone

Published by New Generation Publishing in 2018

Copyright © Rodney Stone 2018

First Edition

The author asserts the moral right under the Copyright, Designs and Patents Act 1988 to be identified as the author of this work.

All Rights reserved. No part of this publication may be reproduced, stored in a retrieval system or transmitted, in any form or by any means without the prior consent of the author, nor be otherwise circulated in any form of binding or cover other than that in which it is published and without a similar condition being imposed on the subsequent purchaser.

www.newgeneration-publishing.com

ON THE 1ST JULY 2016 MY LIFE CHANGED FOREVER!

After years of abusing my body with alcohol and cocaine my life flashed before my eyes, when I was moments from death as I threw up over two pints of blood and was immediately rushed to hospital, where I was diagnosed with oesophageal varices needing six veins band and glued then was also diagnosed with advanced stage four liver cirrhosis! From that night on I never drank, smoked or touched cocaine ever again… MY NAME IS RODNEY STONE.

Chapter One

This journey I am about to take you on is based on my true life events that start from being brought up into a very racially influenced area that made my views, beliefs and thought processes very blinkered until I was able to think straight and begin a different journey onto a new path, and to look at life with a whole different outlook. It will make you laugh, cry and hopefully make you understand that anything in life is possible!

I was born on the 9th October 1976, son to Pat and Les, brother to Nicola, Kelly and Paul. We lived in Brockley, South London. It was a rough multicultural area, we were one of two white families in a street of forty-seven. Back in the 70s early 80s times were so different to how they are these days back then it was skin colour v skin colour even country of origin v country of origin. It was without a doubt a do or die kind of way of life. So with us being in a minority in our area growing up on our street was tough. We had to fight to survive. I have horrible memories as young as the age of five, when there was banging so loud on our front door it felt like the door was going to come off its hinges and when my mum answered it there was a group of at least five African women screaming and shouting in my mums face. Now my mum is a very strong woman who would die protecting her family and home and they could have quite easily done just that this day. As they shouted my mum did no more than a protective lioness protecting her cubs would do shouted back. The next thing I remember is my mum being dragged from our door step and all five of them beating her severely to the point where she was black and blue and they caused her to have a haemorrhage in her stomach. The whole street could hear the screams so everyone came out of their houses, all the womens sons included. As me and my siblings stood screaming and crying watching our mum being tortured the womens sons grabbed me, I was pushed to the floor, hit, bitten and thrown at a car window. I hit it that hard I can still remember the vibrations my body felt on impact! I was only five yet nearly four decades later this event I witnessed still haunts me till this day. My dad was well known in our area and had a large group of well connected friends who heard what had happened to me and my mum, so they all turned up in their cars all tooled up! Due to the severity of what happened next we moved from this area straight away for our own safety.

We moved to Deptford right opposite Deptford park. This is where my love of football took off as I would spend most of my time over there kicking a ball around at every spare opportunity I got. I went to St Joseph's school in Rotherhithe. I loved my new school I even played for their school team. I enjoyed our new area as well, as after witnessing the race wars from a young age I always felt more comfortable playing with only white kids and at this time Rotherhithe was a very white area. Millwall football stadium was only ten minutes walk from my house but as my dad was a fanatic spurs fan as he played for them as a school boy it wasn't until I was old enough to go out on my own that on a Saturday I would walk up to the Den to watch my beloved Millwall play. As a boy I would always go to the Deptford car auctions with my dad on a Tuesday and Thursday and get a cup of Bovril for 50p to keep warm. Then on a Sunday my dad would take me over to Deptford park to play for a local team called Metrocolts, where I started to become a talented footballer. One day when I got in from school, my mum told us she had signed us up to a drama school which I loved and even got picked to play as a main character in a Bugsy Malone production but the rehearsals were on a Sunday so I had to choose between acting and football., I loved both but football won hands down so I had to give drama school up. Although life was going good, as we were starting to put the nightmare of what happened in Brockley behind us all, history was starting to repeat itself when my sister Nicola started to hang about with the wrong crowd and become a problem child, getting into of all sorts of trouble and fights. She came home one day upset that a black girl in her class kept trying to intimidate her. So enough was enough for my mum and dad, they dragged Nicola over to the park and made her stand up to the girl and fight her back. That was how you had to deal with situations in those days because if you didn't stand up for yourself people would walk all over you and your life would be a living hell. My dads brother moved to Welling and could not praise the area enough, so my parents took the decision to move us all to Bexleyheath.

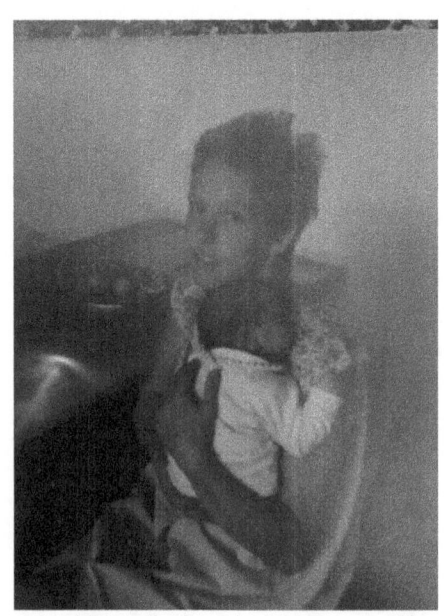

My mum with paul after she came out of hospital

Me, my Mum and brother Paul

Chapter Two

Moving to Bexleyheath was an absolute culture shock for me and my family. I remember my uncle Wilf picking me and my sister Kelly up from school in Rotherhithe to take us to our new house;, my jaw nearly hit the floor in shock at the difference in the area. As crazy as it may seem the fact that there was grass everywhere made Deptford look like a concrete jungle. Me and my older sisters started Welling school none of us knew a single person but all of that soon changed when my love of football introduced me to my mates that have turned into life long friends. It didn't start off all rosey though, as a fight was arranged at Danson park between myself and a now best mate of mine Scott. This resulted in us having a tear up and to this day Scott still laughs about walking into my fist the first time we met. From that day me and Scott have been good friends;, we both followed Millwall with a passion along with our other mates Jim Grogen, Mole, Burak and John Cordier. I always look back and consider myself to be the kid who had everything when we were growing up, especially now I have a family of my own, I can really see and appreciate how hard my mum and dad worked to make sure we never went without. We were a well travelled family who had a holiday every year without fail; we went nice places like Florida, Lanzarote, Gran Canaria, Malta, and Majorca. We also had a caravan in Cambersands, so every weekend we would pack a bag jump in the car and head off straight from school on a Friday for the weekend as well as every school half term throughout the year. I was always a popular kid, often the joker of the group and always had the gift of the gab. I played football every opportunity I had, I was team captain at welling school and was the best player in my year. Outside school I played for longlane. I was their captain too, also player of the year and even got the opportunity to go to Holland with my dad when I was only thirteen and play in a tournament for my team. My dad was always proud of how I played football but I always felt I could not play up to his standards, so I would often tell him a match was being played away when it wasn't as I never wanted to let him down. As sporty and athletic as I was I still had my curious rebellious tendencies from a young age, which looking back in hindsight would be the start of my addictive personality being let out to play. Myself, Scott, Jim, Gary and the rest of our group of boys started off like most other teenagers by smoking cigarettes. We thought we were right top boys as we stood round our local shop smoking our superkings we got for 99p on our lunch break. Then we started experimenting with puff., When we were round Jim Grogans one time we all ate a £5 lump each and chewed it till it looked like dog shit stuck in our teeth as our heads were spinning. We would often carry on our puffing sessions round at Jims house, as this was the place we would all meet up. A thief would have had a field day walking past his house, as his mum Dolly would always have a porch full of trainers and a room full of boys playing the sega mega drive, with the room bonged out as we all chatting stoned jargon till we were all monged out. On a Wednesday and Friday we would all visit Lovel youth centre and hang about down there. We always had our rivals even as young as thirteen, when we used to arrange to fight Bexleyheath youth centre. I suppose it's here my passion for fighting began to ignite within me as i enjoyed the thrill of the violence and the fact I was pretty good at it stood me at a great advantage. By the age of fourteen and fifteen we were travelling to Millwall every Saturday to watch the match and loved the vibe and atmosphere that came with it all. I was still on top form on the pitch too at this age and even as I left school and started my job in the printing trade. Even though I was travelling to Euston North London every day I would still go to football training every Tuesday and play matches on Sundays, come rain or shine football was my life. I even got to play for semi-professional teams like Greenwich borough, Erith Town and Tooting & Mitcham. It's quite safe to say I was buzzing on life at this time. So with life being good and England being in the Euros, 1996 was most definitely the best but also the worst summer of my life. It was around this time that after twenty-four years of marriage my mum and dad got divorced. Although I wasn't a kid because I am really close to both parents this hit my very hard emotionally and mentally, I became really angry at the world. After the BNP book shop in Welling shut down, more and more ethnic groups started to move into a once very non-multicultural area. This opened up mental scars and memories I had suppressed about the race wars I witnessed as a child and I began to rebel in horrible twisted ways such as covering my bedroom walls in swastikas and pictures of Adolf Hitler. I sit now and cringe at myself, even admitting that I even wore a gold chain with a swastika on and at that time I wore it with pride, for me wearing it was a way of me fighting back for all the horrible memories that haunted me that I could not forget from when I was a kid. Although I was feeling broken inside I still put on a brave face and socialised regularly with all my old school mates. All through the Euros me, Scott, Jim, Gary, Ronnie, Curtis, Darren, Mole, Borak and Tony would meet at the Toby in Bexleyheath to watch the game, getting drunk and more often than not, I would start turning up for football practice and matches I had to play in still lagging from the night before. It was around this time that my bad panic attacks started (not that anyone at this time knew what a panic attack was as they were unheard of). They were that bad that my mum would take me to the hospital at least three times a week desperate for answers. I even, on occasions slept at the hospital as I felt safe and was worried that if I left I wouldn't be able to breathe properly. One of my biggest regrets at this time was having trials for Leyton Orient but, due to the amount I was letting my social life get in the way of my training, being angry at the world and trying to work out what the panic attacks were, I didn't make the cut and never got to play for them. I did however get to star in a Nike advert on Hackney Marshes, for Parklife Nike and was totally buzzing to meet football stars like David Seaman, Ian Wright, Robbie Fowler and Eric Cantona. On the last day of filming they drew a raffle which I won, so I got two tickets for the Wembley cup final Chelsea v Middlesbrough. My panic attacks at this time had got so out of hand that doctors sent me for an MRI scan which I waited six months for. As I got undressed the doctor noticed my swastika chain that I wore. His face had dropped and began to look angry then he asked why I had it on. I just blagged it and said my Grandad had bought it back from the war. He angrily asked me to remove it as he himself was Jewish! I just smirked and refused so he threw his pen onto the table and left the room, so I just got up and walked out so I never got the scan or any answers to what my attacks were, all through my own stubbornness and ignorance. So I had to find my own answers to the attacks.

Starting to get a name for myself had its good and bad points., The fact that I always went out with a large group of boys meant that we never went out less than ten handed and was never short of having a laugh. It was around this time I had my first lads holiday, about twenty of us in Magaluf. To say it was mental doesn't even come close; it was full of a lot of drinking, dancing and boys being boys.

Our local boozer was the Moon and Sixpence and the fact it was packed on a Thursday and sold five bottles of beers for a fiver was a bonus. Then from the Moon and Sixpence everyone would go straight to Zens or Déjà Vu and these places were open till the early hours of the morning so the drinks were flowing and the packets of cocaine were rife so our drinking and coke sessions would go on till Sunday even then. Even from this age with the suppressed memories, built up anger and reputation taking off I was always getting into fights. It would not even take a lot for me to kick off. All it would take was an accidental nudge or a disrespectful look off the wrong person and that would be it. A lot of my fights were also sorting out other people's shit and aggro; it was becoming a weekly event and most people's nightly entertainment. One night my cousin Joanne was in the Moon and Sixpence and come over to me upset saying she was getting grief off a few blokes, so I told them to watch their mouth not realising they were there mob handed. So as I went to leave the bouncer warned me they were waiting so it kicked off big time with all these blokes and me and my pals. Although I was sweet with the owner he said I was bringing too much trouble to the pub putting him right in the dairy (bought too much unwanted attention to his pub), so I had to stay away. If I'm being totally honest I used to go out looking for trouble. It was like a release system of anger and I'm not gonna lie, at the time I quite liked the buzz. I would even wear out my most shittiest shirt because I knew at the end of the night it would end up torn and covered in blood. One day I was over Avery hill playing football with a few of the boys when I got a phone call from Scott who was drinking up the Toby He rang 'to tell me that there was a bloke playing pool and he had shot the ball at my sister Kelly and just missed her so me and the boys all jumped in our cars and flew up there. As I went storming in Scott pointed towards the garden to where the bloke that had done it was sitting. I didn't ask any questions, I just ran at him and kicked him straight in the head! His head hadn't even connected with the wall before the whole mob went running out of the pub the toby was cleared within seconds. I wasn't bothered about the Tobys owners response to my outburst as I was already barred from there for using moody tenners. That barring I had to take on the chin cause me and the boys were using them for months without the owner knowing.

After being barred from the Moon and Sixpence I started going to the Polo bar in Bexleyheath more and it wasn't long before my name got well known in there as well, especially when I went in there with a full blown skin head, jeans, Ben Sherman shirt, red braces, beered up and slightly charged up after a few lines when the black DJ comments on the mic "SOME PEOPLE HAVE NO DRESS SENSE" as I walked in!...I didn't humour his comment with a response verbally. I just simply stood starred, smirked at him whilst starring him straight in the eye then in full blown Nazi style saluted like Hitler which went down like a lead balloon. With that the crowd of black blokes put down their drinks and headed towards me. Some may have been intimidated but I wasn't I liked a challenge and even though the odds were stacked against me I wasn't fazed at all. To say it kicked off would be an understatement; the fighting continued all through the pub to outside on the street. There were bodies everywhere as no one was giving up, that was until everyone heard the old bill sirens and ran to avoid being nicked.

Me and the boys 30 years later

Chapter three

Around 1999 was a big turning point in my life. It was safe to say I was at my peak when it came to following football and the violence that came with it. There wasn't a match I didn't watch Millwall play, be it home or away; travelling by car, coach or train, come sunshine, snow or rain me and the boys were there. Even if it meant staying in hotels like when we went places like Nottingham, Bournemouth, Blackpool and Cardiff. We would be there. Although it was all about Millwall and the passion we had for the team. Along with it came the social aspects of meeting the boys arranging meets with the rest of the firm, continuous drinking and ample amount of cocaine flowing non-stop. Then along with the football, drinking and cocaine came the football violence and the buzz I got from arranging meets and releasing the anger that constantly ran through my veins. This was better than any buzz I had ever got from any drink or drugs I had ever consumed. One of my biggest turning points was on August 7th it was the first away game of the season – Millwall v Cardiff so we were all up at silly o'clock meeting, as us boys always did, at Scotts house. Early as it was the boozing had started and the lines of coke were racked up before we had even jumped in the car for the three to four hour drive to arrive in Cardiff for around eleven a.m. As soon as we all met up at our arranged meet the old bill were already there to give us and the rest of the firm a police escort to the town centre and to a barriered off pub for us all to drink in. It is safe to say we were more than mob handed that day. Later reports estimated about seven hundred and fifty of us. Some of the Cardiff firm tried kicking off with us before the game and taunted us all, trying to break through the police barriers as we stood drinking waiting to be escorted to the ground. The police were always more than cautious when it came to Millwall playing, mainly because they knew all us firm were game as fuck and would front any banter being thrown at us from any other supporters or firms. So, as they tried pushing through, a few punches were thrown and it kicked off, but most of us were saving ourselves for the match. So the old bill moved us along and we went straight to Cardiffs ground. There was banter all match and the final score was 1-1. As soon as the final whistle went that was when the carnage began. There was mass fighting everywhere, in and out of the ground. I was covered in blood where I had been hit in the face with a brick. The severity of how much it had kicked off was enough for reporters to be all over it and camera crews reporting on the levels of violence that had erupted. I hadn't realised how wide spread this had become until I got back home into Welling and as soon as got in the Bellegrove everyone was saying, "Fucking hell, Rod you're all over the news!" Then with that my mobile rang and it was my mum saying my nan had rang her worried as she saw me on the news fighting and covered in blood. By the evening my face was on every major news channel from the BBC to Sky news, then by the morning we was in all the newspapers. I'd be lying if I was to say I didn't get a buzz off the mayhem we were involved in cause I did. It's probably this moment that made my mum become a nervous wreck every time I went out, as she never knew what I was going to be involved in next or if she was going to get a phone call saying something bad had happened to me. The sad thing is at this time where I was binge drinking heavily and sniffing stupid amounts of cocaine. I had become really selfish so the impact of what my actions were having on those closest to me still wasn't enough for me to stop doing whatever I wanted to do and whenever I wanted to do it. Even after the uproar of what had happened in Cardiff I was out doing exactly the same thing in my locals when Millwall wasn't playing.

Me on Sky News

Me on Lee Rigby March

One of my most spoke about turnouts was the first fight I had with a UFC fighter Lightning Lee Murray, who later went on to be the brains behind one of the world's most brazen crimes, the greatest cash heist in history. It all started when I was at Zens night club with a few of my mates and on that night I was wearing a long black leather coat. Two black blokes tried mugging me off by asking, "Oi mate, you got any watches on yu?" They soon realised they had tried taking the piss out of the wrong person as I smashed into the pair of them, knocking them both out. Then with that the crowd that had gathered due to the commotion I had caused started stepping aside like the parting of the ocean as if Jesus had just walked in. As I looked through the parted crowd I saw Lee Murray walking towards me. He was a big lump, wearing a white t-shirt with "UNDEFEATED CHAMPION" in black letters across the front. I knew there and then it was gonna kick off between us. Most people put in this confrontational situation would have been worried but not me, I just looked back at him and thought 'FUCK IT, LET'S HAVE IT'. People stood in shook not knowing what to do as we exchanged blows, laying into each other, as neither of us was going to give in and be defeated. Considering he fought professionally and I was just a normal bloke who enjoyed the buzz of having a tear up I didn't do too bad at all cause nobody actually won the fight and we were just pulled off each other by a squad full of bouncers. I was then asked to leave (Mainly cause the bouncers were too scared of Lee to ask him to leave) so I was taken to the back entrance and left that way. It's quite safe to say at that moment I was more than chuffed with myself, as not many people would go toe to toe with a professional fighter like I did. The big downfall now though of me having no fear, meant I had now started a feud with a bloke who is going be pissed off he didn't get a better outcome fighting an unprofessional like myself.

With Euro 2000 starting and football being my life I was not only following Millwall but also the England team. So when England had to play Romania, me and the boys planned our trip to Charleroi. We got to Dover and travelled by Seacat to Ostend and the drinks were flowing non-stop. On board were other English supporters from teams like Tottenham, QPR,. Barnet and Portsmouth and as we were all passionate England supporters the atmosphere was good. We were all sharing different football stories and antics we had all been involved in and by the time we arrived at Ostend we were all in good spirits. From here we had to get a train to Charleroi which took about four hours. Waiting at the arranged meet were over four hundred other Millwall boys. We sat drinking in Belgium and the whole atmosphere was buzzing as everyone waited in hope that England would win as we only needed one point to qualify for the quarter final. Unfortunately this was not to be as Phil Neville gave away a penalty in the last minute so we ended up losing 3-2, This final score did not go down too well at all with all us English fans. Because they were that hyped up expecting a win, the blow of not getting through to the quarter final was enough to make tensions run high and all the English started kicking off. But the mad thing is they didn't kick off with the Romanian supporters, they all kicked off with each other; it was absolutely mental. The Belgian police were not impressed at all. Because of the reputation of hooliganism with the English supporters they were expecting trouble. They wanted us out of Charleroi that bad they packed us into the trains personally, but they had rammed us into the train so tight we were like sardines. We resembled a Bangladeshi train all sweating on each other, it was awful. As we got to Ostend we were all majorly dehydrated after drinking all day then in a ramo sweaty train turn out. It was gone midnight so the old bill said we would have to find an open hotel as everywhere was shut, so about fifty of us broke away from the group hoping to find anywhere open. As we strolled through the street an Irish couple opened a pub window and shouted out "YOU BOYS WANT A DRINK?" With that they opened the doors and let us all in; it was like our prayers had all been answered. Not only did we all get a drink, we all got to carry on boozing, then the rest of the squad we had all left ended up turning up as well so the pub was packed with all us English fans drinking till the sun came up. The atmosphere was electric; you seriously could not have wrote it. It's a memory that will always stay with me and make me smile thinking about it, so what ended up being a disappointing football score was all made better by the vibe set that night by all us English firm being together.

Although it might sound muggy to some cause looking back it does to me now, but by this point in my life my reputation was through the roof. Everywhere I went people knew my name. I couldn't go anywhere without people recognising me, be it whether they wanted to hang about with us, talk to us or just use my name to feel protected when the shit hit the fan for them. It was like being a mini celebrity. The mad thing was, even my brother and sisters couldn't go anywhere without being recognised as 'Rodney Stone's brother or sister. This status drove my sister Kelly mad. She would be blatantly blunt and answer with, "Actually, no I'm KELLY, not Rodneys sister!" That always made me laugh. Around this time I met a girl who I started seeing. I enjoyed my social life and football too much to have time to fit a girlfriend in so I found myself always making excuses not to see her, which didn't go down too well, especially when soon after she announced she was pregnant! I think that all my family had hoped that the prospect of me becoming a dad would slow me down, as my panic attacks were worse than ever I was having at least 3-4 a day. The amount of booze and cocaine I was using through being addicted to socialising and football probably didn't help me prevent these from happening. My son Jack was born on the 9th July 2001 and it was, without a doubt, the proudest moment of my life. Despite how everyone perceived me, they only saw the Rodney Stone that I let them see when I was out. Behind closed doors and those closest to me know that I am a very loyal, honest, protective, loving person who was looking forward to being a father and in later years time proved that I actually am a very good dad and that's not self proclaimed, those are the words of my other children. Although I was more than ready to be a dad, I did not want to settle down and definitely was not ready to and didn't see why I should be in a relationship that I didn't want just to be a dad! Because I thought that would not have been fair or healthy for anyone but I could still have been a good dad as lots of parents are not together and are still great parents individually. This however was not to be, because of the life style I led, with football, socialising and drinking this was all used against me! This was the start of many years of sadness and anger for me because I never felt that I ever done anything that ever deserved me being cut out of my son's life. I have always held my hands up and said yes I drank and used cocaine when I went football or socialised but I never drank around Jack or any other child and definitely never took cocaine when I knew I would be looking after him. So when I fought through the courts to see him they put me in contact centres which infuriated me as I didn't feel I warranted having to be monitored when I was with my son, like the nonses and men who had a history of being violent to women and kids that I had to sit with. All I was ever guilty of was having too much of a party hard life style and because of this I was not allowed near my son. This situation caused me years of anger and upset which I could not deal with and the only coping technique I found was through drinking. It was another tick in my box to why drink became an outlet to cover up the pain and frustration of having a situation out of my control. When I drank it helped me forget.

Where I was drinking to suppress everything that I was dealing with, as it felt at the time this was the only answer, it led me on a downward spiral, emotionally and mentally. I began feeling like I was trapped inside my own head; I only had a negative outlook on everything and anything. Looking back it's hard to see how I coped. I was a complete lost soul, suffering in silence at the risk of looking weak and defeated in anyway by anyone, except for my mum who took me to the doctors where I was diagnosed with depression. I still socialised with friends as often as I could as I loved being out with the boys; it was a way of escaping from being inside my own head alone. Girlfriends came and went because no matter who i had a relationship with I was always happier being single. Even when I did have a girlfriend nothing came in between football and being out with the boys. The only sad thing was that I was very much a mans man; men didn't talk about how they felt or their feelings or deal with anything that had any emotional attachment, so I always had to put on a brave face and still act like good old Rod, the life and soul of the party. The mad thing is I played the role well because I went out every weekend and partied hard. We started drinking in the Wrong 'un pub, which was a good name for the pub considering some of the misfits that drank in there and the Frontier post Bexleyheath and we was always at least 30 handed every weekend without fail. One night I was with a good friend of mine, the late Danny Goddard, and a few others in the Frontier post when a small fight broke out between some people that were in there. I was completely lagging, because at that stage my drinking was becoming more regular and not just binge drinking, and I thought it would be funny to throw a chair into the crowd. Looking back, this was a proper stupid move because we were asked to leave the pub and I was already running out of pubs to drink in because I kept being barred from everywhere as my fighting was getting out of hand. As we were leaving we walked past my already made enemy Lee Murray, who was with two huge geezers; he looked as unimpressed to see me as I was to see him. By the look on his face when we clocked each other you could tell he still hadn't got over the first fight we had, so we began to verbally dig each other out. Looking back in hindsight I should have probably shut my mouth and pretended I hadn't seen him, considering I wasn't in any fit state to potentially front out three blokes built like brick shit houses due to the amount of alcohol I had already consumed. Who was I kidding? I wasn't and never have been the kind of bloke to say nothing; it wasn't in my set-up so my mouth ran away with me. Lee jumped the barrier and ran towards me. As we both swung for each other at the same time I came un stuck as Lee's fist connected whereas mine didn't and as his punch hit my cheek my jaw just shattered. It was later revealed that he had broken my cheek bone in four places. I'm not gonna lie, I was completely stung and it was the first time I had ever been knocked to the floor. Even the nurse in A&E was in complete disbelief that the damage caused to my face was only done with a punch as she had seen the same sort of damage done in fights involving weapons. The next day I woke up feeling like my head had been run over by a train and as my eyes opened as they always did after a heavy night of getting on it, the horrors of the night before began to set in. I was meant to be going to watch Millwall v Oldham and go on a BNP march but as I turned up to meet the boys at the café they all stood in shock with their jaws hitting the floor at the state of my face. I pretty much resembled the Elephant Man himself. Gary said, "Rod, mate, you can't go Millwall looking like that!" So Gary stayed with me why the others headed off to watch the match and me and Gal went and met Scott at the Gordon Arms in Chislehurst for a beer instead.

I suppose, given the fact I was drinking too much, sniffing too much, and being barred too much it should have probably encouraged me to calm down a bit. Did it bollocks. I didn't scare off that easily I still cracked on doing what I did best and that was to drink, sniff and socialise to hide from the depression I was suffering from in silence. I went out fighting when I wanted to release the anger I was building up by not dealing with my problems. I was ignoring these problems by drinking . It was becoming impossible to go out drinking without being asked to leave before I had even entered a pub. The same security firm ran all the doormen on all the pubs and they radioed through to let each other know I was en route. So now the feuds I was having were with all the doormen! One night I got on a designated bus that went straight to Déjà Vu nightclub in Swanley with my mates when eight carloads of bouncers followed me there and were after my blood due to a previous incident that had got out of hand. It was only me getting the heads up from the bouncer in Déjà vu, who warned me they were all waiting for me, that saved my bacon. Because there were so many of them he had no other option than to call the old bill and get me escorted home. As I walked out I saw the eight car loads of blokes all standing there in their green bomber jackets waiting for me. I can see why he had to make that decision because that is a situation that would have seriously one hundred percent got out of hand.

Chapter four

As my depression got worse my panic attacks continued and my poor mum was at her wits end not knowing what to do to help me. We had been to doctors and hospitals but even the doctors were baffled as to what to do as I had already been prescribed anti-depressants. So my GP decided to send me for counselling. I went to my one-on-one sessions every Saturday morning to try and see if there was anything they could do to help ease the mental torture I put my mind through every day. I continued my sessions for over six months but I have got to say, I honestly think they made my depression worse. The problem I found was that the counselling sessions made me speak about memories and situations I had suppressed so deep, that when I spoke about them it felt like I was re living everything I was mentally running from and drinking to deal with. So then the pattern would start again; because I would speak about it and re live it, when I left the counsellors I would go straight to the pub to then drink twice as much as I did before to re-suppress it and so the pattern dominoed again. The mental pattern of re-live, re-suppress and re-drink was like a Bermuda triangle in my brain with my mental wellbeing spinning around and around with me stuck in the middle with my silent voice screaming out for help as I was slowly losing all control.

My mum has always tried to do everything she could to help me through all I had to deal with and it wasn't until I looked back on my life with an un selfish head on my shoulders that I realised how hard it must have been for her to watch me destroy myself right in front of her eyes. Especially after everything she had been through and was still going through whilst still trying to help me. My mum was one of six children and had four brothers and one sister. My mum herself was never really a drinker although she had grown up around drink as her dad was a drinker. Her mum was prone to a Guinness but nothing extreme like her dad who died of brain cancer at the age of forty-two, when my mum was only fifteen years old. Leaving my nan to raise six kids alone. My mum was really close to her brothers and sister. When I was only eight years old my Mums youngest brother, Cornelius (Connie) started suffering from fits that he'd never had before. He was only seventeen and got diagnosed with multiple sclerosis. So my Nan wrapped him up in cotton wool and cared for him every day as he slowly, over the next ten years, started to deteriorate. It was heart breaking for our family watching him get admitted Lewisham hospital, where our whole family took over the whole ward, spending every last minute with him that they could, until sadly, two days later, he passed away at the young age of twenty-nine. I was only eighteen at the time and it was awful watching my poor Nan having to bury her own child, that's something no Mum should ever have to do. This event broke my mum as well. She found it so hard to cope with it that it caused her to have a mental break down and she was admitted into Maudsley hospital because the pain was just too much for her to bear. This was the start of a series of heart breaking events that our family had to cope with. A few years later my mums other brother, Johnny was left heart broken when he got divorced from his wife. Johnny had always loved a drink but this made him hit the bottle even harder. He moved in with my Nan for a while before getting his own flat and my Nan would ring my Mum upset, saying she was worried about him because he was drinking more but trying to hide it. She would hear him in the fridge at all hours of the night opening cans. Things got even worse for him when he was living in his flat on his own as he did what a lot of people did and that was to turn to alcohol to help him cope. My Nan rang my mum one day saying she was worried as Johnny hadn't been feeling well all week and she hadn't heard from him in a few days, so she asked my Mum if she would go and check in on him. My mum said she would and asked me to go with her so I did. As I started to knock and not get a response, worry started to set in. We started to call through the letter box, trying to convince ourselves that he might just be asleep but it was when we noticed the door was locked from the inside our stomachs sunk. Still, with no answer the reality that everything was not OK began to set in even more. With that I rang the police and told them about our concerns so they quickly arrived and gained entry into the flat. It was at this moment that our worse fears had been confirmed and it's a moment I will never forget till the day I die. My poor uncle Johnny was lying on his sofa completely yellow, with blood dripping from his mouth, surrounded by empty beer cans everywhere. It was here that he died. He was only forty-six. Later autopsy reports confirmed the cause of death was liver cirrhosis. My poor mum fell to her knees as the tears streamed from her eyes and her heart broken cries wailed through the flat. I just remember the room was spinning as I tried thumbling about trying to find my phone to ring my aunty Linda. As Lindas phone answered she passed me straight to my Nan I could feel my heart crumbling as my lips began to move to tell my Nan what had happened. It was the worst phone call I have ever had to make in my life and if I close my eyes I can still hear the heart breaking screams that my Nan bellowed out as I was telling her that her son Johnny was dead. So, yet again, our family had to watch my Nan bury another one of her sons. My uncle William (Wilf) was a complete rock for my Nan and family. He organised and arranged the funeral to try and make things as bearable for my Nan as possible. After losing two sons my mum and aunty Linda took my Nan under their wing and took her everywhere with them to make she was OK and try to lift her spirits as much as they could. My uncle Wilf only lived round the corner so he would keep an eye on her when he could too. Wilf always had his own health issues and experienced breathing problems which was due to a rupture in his throat that he got when he was born. This was caused by the incompetence of a nurse who fucked up when clearing mucus from his throat after my Nan had delivered him, causing him a lifetime of problems. It was later revealed that he was advised to have an operation as it was life threatening but no one knew this until it was too late. As his health issues started to worsen and Wilf became unwell my Nan kept an eye on him to make sure he was OK, until one night when they had all gone home my aunt Linda got a phone call from Wilfs girlfriend telling her Wilf had passed away. My Nan Mum and Linda rushed straight round to his house where yet again police confirmed he had died; he too was only forty-six. This caused massive devastation to everyone. My late uncle Ian sanwell was like a rock to my mum and Linda as tragedy upon tragedy was all too much for them to cope with. I had not only lost another uncle, but my mum had lost another brother and my poor Nan had lost yet another son. My Nan by now, had lost three sons in ten years; she had them all buried together in Hither Green. To say she was a broken woman does not even come close. Her heart was broken, her soul was destroyed and her life was never to be the same. It was soul destroying for not only myself but my mum watch my poor Nan become a shell of the woman she was before. My Nan never ever got over losing her boys; one child is hard but three in ten years don't even bear thinking about. My Nan started to have health issues so my mum was always taking her to and from Lewisham hospital as she got diagnosed with lung cancer which eventually spread to her liver. My mum and Linda brought her home to care for her and spend every last minute with her, until she sadly took her last breath a week and a half later. Losing my Nan hit us all really hard; she was the heart of our family and the hole that was left when she went has never been filled.

I cannot begin to imagine how on earth my Mum ever coped losing three brothers and her mum in just over a decade. These sort of tragedies don't often happen to people in a lifetime, let alone a decade. I can't even begin to imagine the pain that she feels inside, carrying what she has been through around with her every day. What's more, no matter what my mum was going through and, as her life shows, she has definitely been through more than most, she never once gave up on me even when I was giving up on myself and she always helped me as much as she could probably when she didn't even the strength to cope herself. It's not until later years when I looked at what I have put my mum through that I can actually see how unknowingly selfish I have been throughout my life. This was all due to alcoholism and cocaine abuse because all the time my mum was being there for me I really should have been there for her a lot more than I was.

Chapter five

When I look back and try to think of a time that my drinking started to get out of control I can't really put my finger on any one thing specifically, other than me always using drink as a comfort, support system and a cure, which obviously is definitely not the way to deal with life at all. The first time I can ever remember seeing alcohol in this way was when my panic attacks were really bad. I was suffering from them at least three or four times a day and I was talking to my brother-in-law, Stuart about it and how they were getting me down. It just so happened that my anxiety was through the roof on this day and Stuart passed me a beer and said, "Here, drink this, it will calm you down and sort you right out!" You know what, it did! Where my panic attacks were that bad, to have something that eased the anxiety that took over my body like it did at that point, felt like someone was watching down on me from up above and cured me! So from then on, every time I could feel my heart start to palpitate, my throat start to tighten and my brain start to race as the panic attack was kicking in, I would neck a beer. So yet again alcohol ticked another box in my brain to why I justified to myself it was a good thing. I had managed to convince myself that alcohol comforted the anxiety, was a support system for my anxiety and, at that point, I thought it cured my anxiety. I could not have been more wrong, I just did not realise it at that time of my life. All I could see was the fact that I enjoyed drinking and it eased my attacks so for me it was a win-win situation. Even my family couldn't pin point a time they thought I might have an alcohol addiction. Because all through my teens and into my twenties all I was doing was what all the other boys were doing and that was going out and getting on it it's what everyone done. So how was I meant to notice anything any different? If anything, my family was more worried about the amount of cocaine and other drugs I was experimenting with. I never saw anything I was doing as being a problem; all I was doing was being one of the boys, having a laugh and not even considering the consequences of my actions. I would be lying if I was to say we didn't have some of the best and funniest times of our lives being out of our nut; you couldn't begin to make-up some of the antics we got up to. I mean how many people in the history of being sober have ever sat in a room with their mates colouring in a Dalmatian's spots in with Tipp-Ex? I can't imagine there are many out there, that's for sure! My mate Burn's mums face was a picture coming home to her now pure white Dalmatian though. She looked nearly as confused that night as she did the night we were all sitting in her house completely off our trolleys and that paranoid we all buried our cocaine in her garden. It seemed like an absolutely wicked idea at the time, that was until we was roasting for another line, so we had to try and route round the garden commando style in the hope that his mum wouldn't hear us and wake up while we were digging about trying to remember where we buried it. One time on February $14^{th}$the day of the year when men should be thinking about taking their missus out and being romantic, but no, not us boys we were in Brighton by 1.30 on a pub crawl till we got to Brightons football ground, to watch our real love Millwall play. We were drinking all day so by the time the half time whistle went we was roasting for another beer, but the bar was ramo with supporters. We couldn't even get close which made tensions run high., Shouting got louder and people started kicking off but it was over as quickly as it started as the old bill was all over it. I got CS gassed so my eyes felt like they were on fire and i was struggling to see as I went into the toilets to try and wash out the flames that were melting my eyeballs. I cracked on trying to watch the match with what eyesight I had left and the final score ended up being 1-1. So we all headed back to the coach where a supply of drink awaited us for the journey home, only problem we had now was that the cocaine had run out so everyone was clucking for a sniff. A phone call was made and we got the coach driver to pull into Clackets Lane service station where we somehow managed to pull off a deal and got more wraps dropped off to us. From the smile on every ones faces anyone would have thought we just pulled out a winning lottery ticket instead of a pocket full of packets the way there faces were all beaming from ear to ear, when we got back on the coach. All the way home you could have probably still heard us all from Brighton singing and chanting with the words "OI OI WE GOT OUR PACKETS AT CLACKETS". At least that night we all left together, not like the day Millwall were playing Notts County and all of us were on it hard the night before which obviously meant we had zero minutes sleep and carried on drinking as we travelled up and met the rest of the Millwall boys at our arranged meet at Hooters in Nottingham. We carried on sniffing and drinking till we were completely hammered to the point our mate Martin passed out in the chair. So us boys thought we'd help keep him warm and wrapped him to the chair in toilet roll from head to toe before all leaving to watch the match. We weren't completely heartless though because we made sure we didn't cover his mouth so he could still breathe., not like us, we could hardly breathe at all through laughing so much. So with some of these events being just a drop in the ocean of mad turnouts we got up to whilst being out of our nuts, it's no wonder my family were starting to worry about my cocaine intake rather than my alcohol abuse. Looking back in hindsight, I was always on it more than I realised because the reality was real, I did have a problem more than I was willing to own up to. The realisation of this hit me full pelt in 2011 when one Friday afternoon after a week of drinking and amples amount of cocaine, because at this time I had it on tap. This Friday started like any other Friday with me wishing the days of the week away, knowing the Friday feeling will be hitting all the boys as well. My phone was alight all afternoon with phone calls arranging our plans on where to go first and sorting out who needed gear and who was already sorted. So I started off by making sure I looked the part by going into Welling to get my hair cut and on the way there I didn't feel right at all. I kept on getting breathless but at the time I thought it was nothing more than a panic attack. As I was meeting my brother and Joe at the Turnpike for a beer after my haircut I just thought I'd ride it out till I got to the pub, where I necked a beer, racked up a line and sniffed it thinking that would sort my head out!?! 'THAT WOULD SORT MY HEAD OUT??' who was I trying to kid?? Looking back, it's those sort of unjustified and irrational solutions to real situations that should have opened my eyes to addressing the fact I was an addict, but no, that would have been too much of a hard path to follow and definitely was not a path I felt I needed to even contemplate at the time. So, with that in mind I carried on my night in true Rodney Stone style, by putting a smile on my face but inside I felt like shit. So we did no more than call on more gear and as my phone rang, I walked across the road to the car where I was about to make a deal, when my right arm all of a sudden felt like a lead weight with pains in my chest and back and every cell of my body felt like it had been run over by a train, I had honestly never felt anything like it, It was the worst feeling of illness I had ever experienced in my life. I tried as hard as I could to put on a normal face, continued my deal and walked back into the pub fully loaded with packets and ordered a round of Strongbows. I stayed out having more beers and sniffing more lines, until I couldn't physically stay out any longer as the feeling of being unwell was all too much, even as strong faced as I was I had to go straight to my mums. I told my mum I wasn't feeling well and had to go and lie down. I had the most restless night ever and could not settle for love nor money, by now the pain was really severe in my back, neck, chest and even my jaw ached like crazy. My mum was that worried about me she drove me straight to the hospital where they done ECG's and chest x-rays that were showing normal signs but then a blood test they done confirmed the worst. With that I was moved to a private ward where two nurses and one doctor gave me an injection of warfarin and rushed me into the critical care unit, where they finally told me that I had been having a heart attack for two days. I was immediately given more medication through cannulas that had been inserted into my hands and was wired up to monitors and told I would be monitored for 24hrs then I would be going straight into have heart surgery the following day. As my mum sat beside me being told what was happening, with every word that was being spoken by the doctor it destroyed her more and more, I could literally hear her heart crumbling into bits as she rang my Dad in Spain to tell him the devastating news. On the morning of my surgery I honestly thought my life was over. This feeling was made a million times worse when I was handed a consent form and asked to sign it to confirm that I knew the risks that go along with heart surgery and that they had made me aware that 1 in 200 people have complications during the procedure I was about to have. Part of me didn't even want to sign anything, I just wanted it all to go away and have been a bad dream! I mean, how on earth had this happened? And why me? Less than 48hrs previous I was in a pub necking beers thinking I was indestructible! I was only thirty-five. I should not have been lying there; these sort of things only happened to other people and as for heart attacks, they only happened to old people, didn't they? How wrong and naïve had I been? I was lying there and for the first time ever that I could remember I actually felt vulnerable. As I left the ward to go down to surgery I'm not ashamed to admit the tears were rolling down my face. Because not only did I have to witness the fact that I had made my mum cry uncontrollably but also for the fact this was the first time I had not only felt vulnerable but I was more scared than I had ever been in my life! As I was wheeled into the room ready for surgery there were six surgeons and cardiologists waiting in there all dressed in their green overalls waiting for me. The butterflies were fluttering like anything through my stomach. They numbed my wrist so they could go through the main artery, my arm was in a vice as they inserted blue dye into the artery to show them a clearer picture of which arteries needed stents and balloons to help them open up. My arm went ice cold as they were explaining to me what they were doing all through the procedure. I had a monitor in front of me taking pictures of my heart as they inserted four stents and balloons into my thinning arteries that were causing my heart to be starved of oxygen. I was in surgery for over two hours and after surgery I was speaking to Dr Patel and he was asking me about my life style, so I began to tell him quite honestly about my liking of alcohol and cocaine. I was worried he might judge me and look down on me as a person. The mad thing is, as much as an amazing cardiologist as he is, he didn't judge me one bit. He did however explain that it is uncommon at thirty-five to have suffered a heart attack, but even more uncommon to have a heart failure. This caused all my arteries on the left side of my heart to be blocked, it's here that he confirmed all of this was due to my party hard life style. I was in hospital for eleven days and began to take my medication of 25 tablets a day on the cardiology ward, where I was by far the youngest on there by at least thirty years to all the other patients. I had lots of visitors daily between my mum, sisters, brother, aunt, uncle and even my friends Tony, Scott, Stuart and Gary who I had obviously scared very much. It was this life changing event that really made me question and change all my narrow minded, shallow, blinkered and sometimes racist views of other people of different races that I had held for so many years because of the events that scarred me, after watching what my mum and family went through when I was only five. I had spent so many years filling my mind with hatred due to this, yet the very same people I had convinced myself I needed to hate were the same people that were here operating on me and caring for me in order to save my life, when I had spent so many years destroying myself due to un resolved issues I kept inside, creating the monster I had become. When I left the hospital I was adamant that I had to turn my life around, I actually felt relieved inside that I would never sniff cocaine again. For the next two months I stayed at my mums to start a new life. I changed my diet, I stopped smoking, I even started to exercise to try my hardest to stay as healthy as I could, everyone noticed a change in me. My mum wouldn't let me out of her sight just in case I relapsed and ended up back in hospital. At this time I really didn't think I would ever relapse, because surely being that close to death would be a wakeup call for me?... surely feeling that scared and vulnerable would be a wakeup call?... surely watching my mum lose three brothers, her mum and nearly her son would be a wakeup call?... surely after all those years of having panic attacks, worrying that I was having a heart attack and now I had ACTUALLY had a heart attack was enough to be a wakeup call?..... OR would it?

Unfortunately not! On December 17th I got invited to a school reunion at the Coach and Horses in Bexley and I started off with all good intentions, especially as I knew how worried my friends were after what had happened to me so I started off by having just a couple of lager tops then, before I knew it, I was ordering strongbows. My mates began to really get concerned as I was asking them for a line out of their cocaine. They were horrified I was even contemplating indulging in it and I was there horrified that weren't even contemplating giving me any. It was fine by me though because I did no more than make a call to order my own two packets of gear but made sure I didn't let any of them know I had it. I just kept sneaking in and out of the toilet on my own hoping that my secret would go un noticed. As crazy at it may seem, in just an instant all that I went through in hospital seemed like a distant memory as I had convinced myself I was ok now, I hadn't been ill, I was leading a better lifestyle, all of the vulnerability and fear that I felt in hospital had gone so I was convinced a few beers and a couple of packets would be ok! My friends weren't silly, they knew exactly what I was up to so none of them would let me go back to their houses with them as they were annoyed that I could have been that selfish and they were right. When I got back to my mums wired out of my brain, I got the beers out of the fridge to drink continuously to try and help me not only sleep but also just pass out as I was consumed with so much self regret due to the guilt and hatred I felt towards myself after what I had just done after all I had been through and I knew that in the morning when I woke up on a come down I would hate myself even more as the horrors of what I was doing to myself would set in and take control and so the cycle would start again.

Chapter six

Looking back at the rollercoaster of destruction that was my life I noticed it was here that I should have used my head and been strong enough to make the changes necessary to stop poisoning not only my body, but my mind and my mental and emotional health as well. I'm sure a majority of the population going through what I did would have looked at the life they were leading and had led and would have valued their very existence more. For some reason I seemed to rebel against the situation and stupidly do the complete opposite. In doing this I began to slowly start alienating myself, as people were angry at the fact they were the people closest to me and they had watched me nearly lose my life, so in the process had been to hell and back with me. Yet here I was selfishly throwing all their concern, love and support straight back in their faces by carrying on still drinking. So they did no more than stop associating themselves with me and knowing what I know now, I don't blame them one bit for doing so. How my family coped with the addictive life I led I will never know. How I had the audacity to still look my mum in the face when she took me back to the GP because she was concerned about me, that even the GP said my life style was putting my already damaged heart at more risk. I can't believe that the pain of what I was putting my family through was not strong enough to impact on the self-guilt that ate away at me, which just shows the power of my addiction! I like many other addicts, thought I knew better than everyone else, so how could I possibly care about anyone else's feelings when I didn't care enough about myself to even take my medication! Even when I got rushed to hospital again with chest pains and had to be monitored to make sure it was not another heart attack, I cared just enough about myself to get paranoid about touching cocaine for a while. As for drinking I did what all addicts do and that was to look at my addiction with tunnel vision, so I enabled myself to justify that what I was doing was ok. At that time I saw nothing wrong with still having a drink, even though my GP had advised I was still putting myself at risk. I had convinced myself I wasn't because I had cut out the cocaine for a while and was only drinking. I had justified it to myself that I was doing a good thing because it was cocaine that would put my heart at risk but drinking wouldn't put my heart under pressure. It sounds absolutely crazy now even contemplating this would be ok and how scary it is that an addictive trait can mentally lead your mind into making decisions that would put the rest of your body and life at risk. Once again this proves the power of addiction. My mum did all she could to try and help me with my drinking and cocaine use and my GP even referred me to a drink and drug counsellor who I saw twice a week. The counsellor even said I had the highest tolerance levels he had ever seen someone have, but the more he spoke about drinking the more I wanted one. I didn't feel we were getting anywhere. Even after going to this group, then getting referred to another group, I just could not get to grips with how they were trying to tackle my problems with me. Personally I found their programmes and teachings too text book and their strategies were no a vale to me, as they had no personal experience on addictions dependency. So all the talking in the world from these people would never have given me enough structure to make myself mentally strong enough to face my addictions and prepare myself for a life of sobriety. In fact the more I went and got nowhere the worse I got. It was as if I had condemned myself as irreparable, which made me self-hate more, which led to me drinking heavier. The ironic thing was that I was punishing myself for not being able to stop drinking by drinking more to block out what I could not change, which is irony on another level! I drank so much one night that when my mum came round to see me she let herself in because I was barely conscious, so I couldn't even get to the door. Obviously, after her bad experience with her brother, she drove me straight to A&E where I got accessed by psychiatrists, drink and drug counsellors and doctors who were all in agreement that I was in danger of putting my life at risk. Due to my mental state of mind I wasn't really aware of what was going on. I was however sent to Woodlands psychiatric unit but as it was 1am on a Sunday morning there were no beds ready straight away, so I was put in a communal recreational area where I was left lying on the sofa. I can remember lying staring into space not really grasping the seriousness of the situation and position I was in. I was lying motionless, gagging for another beer, but every time I moved my eyes I was hallucinating and I kept on hearing my mums voice calling me but every time I looked to see if she was there all I was surrounded by was black space and empty chairs. This left me feeling like a fly caught in a spider's web, as I lay solely on my own not knowing what was going on wondering or where the hell I was until I feel asleep. Times like these proves that drink and drugs all seem like fun and games until we watch someone we love become someone we don't know! It was there I stayed until I was woken up by voices and other patients who stood staring gormlessly at me through the window. I still hadn't realised at this point that I had actually been sectioned. I was given a room where I had a shower and was offered a breakfast, not that I ate it as I had no appetite at all. I was just sat on the bed in the room on my own until a doctor and psychiatrist came in to speak to me to explain what was going on. First of all I was told that I had been sectioned for my own safety, then that I would be doing a detox programme that consisted of an injection of vitamins that had to go in my bum cheek and a daily dosage of Librium. They explained that this medicine was used as a sedative for hypnotic medication that was used for anxiety, insomnia, and withdrawal from drink and drugs and whilst I was in there I would be having one to one counselling for the 72 hour sectioning. We wasn't allowed any phones or chargers, due to the risk of trying to commit suicide, but the fact we were still allowed our dressing gown belts seemed to make that rule totally contradictory. I wasn't allowed my medical dosette boxes obviously again due to the risk of suicide, so I had to wait for all my medication and receive it one by one like Jack Nicholson during medication time in One Flew Over the Cuckoo's Nest. I got to meet some of the other patients who were all in there for mental health issues from anxiety, bipolar, schizophrenia and other serious mental health issues. I was the only patient sectioned for addiction detox. This fact made me feel even more on my own and at rock bottom, that I had allowed my once party life style to spiral into a life of addiction and loneliness surrounded by people who I would have never dreamt that I would have been associated on the same level with. Yet here I was in the same boat, feeling helpless, not only for myself, but also for these poor patients who were solely on their own, struggling to keep their lives together with no one visiting them and no family to help them and no support system at all. I felt awful when my family visited me because I didn't feel I deserved to have them there for me when it was due to my own self destruction that I was in this position in the first place! Then here were these poor people who had genuine illnesses through no fault of their own with absolutely no one. After the 4th day I was eventually allowed out of the premises to walk to the shop if I wanted to, so I used this time to help other patients out and get them things like tobacco and newspapers. It wasn't much but when you're that rock bottom, stuck inside your own head suffering like a lot of the other patients were, these little acts of kindness like token gifts meant the world to them. Their faces lit up like a kids does on Christmas morning when seeing their presents waiting to be opened. It was as if just for that split second, they had a hint of hope in their eye when receiving my help that they knew someone actually cared enough to think about them. I did however find it beyond bizarre that the medical staff wanted to keep me in there longer as they feared I would easily relapse this soon, yet here they were allowing me to go to the shop? Realistically I could have easily bought a drink or called on some gear on any of those trips to the shops but they didn't seem to question that? I did however, whilst I was in there, use my addiction experience and counselling session knowledge to try and interact with other patients who I really felt for. They themselves were so grateful for the time I spent with them listening and talking to them; they really opened up to me and openly admitted that my support helped them more than the trained professionals that worked there. I was on the Librium for five days but spent eleven days in there all in all and when they asked if I was ready to leave I agreed I was and so was let home which felt good. I was however apprehensive on how I would cope staying sober being back in my own normal surroundings and hoped that I would still get the aftercare support from the psychiatric unit, as they assured me I would on being discharged. I tried to settle in to a life without addiction but it was really hard. So I started to focus on getting some sort of normality and structure back to make me feel like the man I was before I become a shadow of who I once was, before I spiralled into somebody I don't recognise anymore. I started to try and get some sort of access to my son Jack again and contacted my solicitor, who then contacted the courts, who then contacted Cafcass. The pressure of having to relive the pain of being disregarded from my sons life was like a repeated dagger in my heart. I tried my upmost not to turn to drink and stayed sober for over two months but when I had a hair strand test done for court, it came back positive as it was a six month strand test. I tried everything to convince the powers that be that I really had been trying to turn my life around and had not been drinking or taking cocaine, and really was willing to do all it took to be able to be an active part of my sons life, to make up for all the lost years I had already had stolen from me. Yet again this was not be because yet again, I had strangers judging me who didn't even know me, who only had the opinion of people who were trying to keep my son from me. Just because they were in a position of authority they had the power to not even give me a chance to be the parent I longed to be. It was beyond soul destroying trying my hardest to fight a forever losing battle. What was worse was through my whole life I always fought hard in every situation and what was killing me the most was this situation with my son was one battle I was always going to lose but wanted to win the most. The frustration and anger this caused me inside tore me apart, broke my heart and destroyed me every single day. Even after everything I had gone through this was not enough to be able to stop using drink and cocaine as my coping technique to block out the feeling of emptiness and frustration that bubbled away inside me every day. When I was gambling with my life through my addiction I would start self-hating more so ended up hitting it harder, then would self-detox. I would even research drink and drugs to try and get a better understanding; to see if there was anything I could find out that I didn't already know, to help motivate my brain to stop relapsing, every time I found the power to beat the addictions that wore me down. Every time I stopped it would only ever be weeks at a time. All the whole time I was making myself that ill I even got diagnosed with diabetes. On diagnoses my GP told me this type 2 diabetes was bought on purely through alcohol abuse. Not only did I have my own health problems that should have raised alarm bells for me to be strong enough to stand up to my addiction, but I also lost my really good friend, Christian Mears. He too battled a life of addiction just like myself; he was even strong enough to move to a completely different area to get away from all triggers to help himself get his life back and so stayed with his dad. Unfortunately it was all too late for him as he passed away at a young age of forty. The Cause of death was alcohol related! This bought back so many bad memories of when my uncle died in exactly the same way and both had their lives robbed from them so young. It was all through the poison that is so readily available every day and in every shop you go in, that killing poison being alcohol! Me and my mates all took this really hard. He was our second mate in two years that had passed away; the first friend took his own life after struggling with depression. The maddest thing was although we suffered the pain of losing close friends and watching how it destroyed, not only us but their families, the pain and anguish still was not enough to stop every single one of us still getting on it. In fact although I was the main one who most definitely should have taken on board what was happening right in front of my eyes what with having my heart attack, being diabetic, losing access to my son, then the deaths of my uncle and two friends with the main cause in every one of these situations being addiction I should have run a mile and never touched drink or drugs again but no, I didn't. What a mug I was because I hit it even harder than I did before. It was as if my brain literally had no other coping technique at all other than alcohol. It wasn't even the fact of drinking for fun and socialising anymore because I was becoming more depressed to the point where I was drinking more behind closed doors. I had even stopped going to Millwall. All that had happened played on my mind daily and I struggled every time I thought about it. so I, yet again, justified a tick box in my head to let this poison keep being my solution. It was knowing when to stop once I started as well. One weekend I was up the Great Harry pub drinking, doing what I do best and that was putting a smile on my face and acting like an ostrich by putting my head in the sand and pretending my life was ok. That was until I had severe stomach pains and rushed to the bathroom, sat on the toilet and passed through loads of blood, which obviously scared the shit out of me. I couldn't even tell my mates as I was too embarrassed to mention anything that personal, so I kept it to myself until I saw my mum, who took me straight to the doctors the next day. I was sent straight to the hospital where I remained in isolation for five days. Here I was, again not only putting my poor mum through the turmoil of having to rush me to hospital yet again, but also putting my already weakening body through so much self-destruction through my addictions, that dominoed onto weakening my already fragile mind as I lay over thinking, whilst self-hating knowing I had, yet again, failed myself and now caused more damage to another part of my body. The damage I had caused raised red flags on my liver. Red flags are a warning that you are causing damage to your liver causing it to be unable to function properly. So now through no self-control I had destroyed myself even further! It is a bad situation to be in relying on alcohol for your acceptance because then you start doing things that aren't acceptable. When was this going to end? How was this going to end? Surely now I could use all the intelligence I had into motivating my mind into making the right decision before I too lost my own life!

Chapter seven

With me destroying not only myself but everything in my life, I was now at a cross roads where I had to decide which way to go forward . On one hand, I desperately needed help to stop my pattern of self-destruction that was my life, yet on the other hand, all the help and support I had already been given had been wasted on me. As all I had done was abused every inch of it by letting myself down and everyone around me. In the process, the only choice I now felt I was left with was to distance myself and break contact with my friends and family to try and get myself straight on my own. I did honestly feel at the time that this was the right thing to do as every time I looked at my mum I could see that the impact that I was having on her was not good. I just felt I was bringing everyone down. So when I got offered a flat in Lewisham I took it and although this was not somewhere I would chosen to have lived I knew I would be out of everybody's way. Deep down I was hoping this was what I needed to start again and hopefully re-find myself. Due to my health problems, depression and alcoholism I had been signed off work so i just concentrated on doing my flat up and making it as homely as I could. To be fair, I didn't really mind the area once I was there. I quite enjoyed the location as I was right by the market so the area was always busy. If I did start to feel isolated I would venture out, even if it was to just walk through the high street to get a paper and enjoy people watching and would lap up the atmosphere of the hustle and bustle around me. I was also near all public transport routes so I started to get back in contact with other groups of people I knew. I even ended up buying fishing rods and equipment, even though I've never fished in my life, as it never interested me. But as I was meeting up with a life-long pal of mine, Frazer who went fishing regularly I thought I would try it and use this as a new avenue to pursue. Even more so because of all the hype people give it and would say how enjoyable and therapeutic it was. It seemed the ideal hobby I should try and get into in order to help assist me in my rehabilitation. Unfortunately however it turned out to be the most short lived idea I've ever had. All I ended up doing was sitting there bored out my head, agitated and pissed off I couldn't get home because I was sat stuck at a lake with no transport and freezing cold! So it was safe to say that idea went straight out the window. I was desperately trying to find ways to lead a normal life, whatever normal is meant to be? All I knew was that after everything I had been through, all that I already put my body through and mostly all I put my family through, all I wanted to do was get back some normality without dictation from addiction ruling my head and life. For me, all the time addiction had a hold of me it was dictating the course of my life. As when I was drinking and using cocaine I had to start hiding my addiction more and the more I took the more I couldn't stop and in the process the more people I pushed away therefore isolating myself more. I truly thought that by trying to go it alone I was making it easier for everyone to not have to deal with or worry about me. It wasn't until my Mum and sister Kelly came to see me after not seeing me for a while I realised my poor Mum was worrying herself to death not having me around or hearing from me. So while I thought I was doing the right thing staying away it would seem all the hurt I thought I was protecting my family from was doubled doing it the way I did. Christmas was approaching and the thought of me being by myself was destroying my mum, especially due to the fact she knew this was a time of the year I struggled with most, as to me it was another Christmas I hadn't spent with my son. Seeing how upset and worried my mum and sister were I agreed to spend Christmas and New Year at my Mums house. I managed to have my first sober Christmas I'd had in years, which was still hard given the fact people were still indulging around me. Which although hard, I had to accept, as it was all of their Christmas and New Year's

Eve as well. It was the start of a new year and I was already starting the year ahead with a fresh state of mind and feeling optimistic. I tried to keep myself as busy as I could, even if that meant some days just walking through the market talking to the stall holders and generally watching life pass me by. I'm not gonna lie, each day was getting harder and harder but I did manage to stay clean for fourteen weeks, but isolating myself with distance from all my support network was only good for a short term basis. I found the more time went on the harder it became for me to stay focused on my goal of sobriety of freedom from addiction. It was not even the fact that I didn't have the will or want to make and keep a better life for myself because I think, looking back, I can only remember never really seeing the seriousness of the situation that I was in, it's only now looking back in hindsight that at this time in my life, I can only ever remember thinking the lifestyle I was living was not as bad as everyone was telling me it was which is an absolutely crazy thought process to have, especially given the fact that I had already had a heart attack and had red flags on my liver, yet still I was only ever really stopping what I was doing to please everyone else rather than myself. It's probably this channel of thought that allowed me to relapse every time. This was even more apparent when one morning, after nearly four months, I woke up bored and for no reason at all walked to the shop in the rain, and bought two bottles of vodka then called on some gear. It wasn't even as if I had anyone coming to drink and sniff with me because I was sitting at home doing it by myself hiding my addiction behind closed doors, and self-hating as the pattern of my lifestyle repeated itself. Though I could never see the seriousness of my behaviour, every time I sat indoors worrying what people closest to me would think if they knew I relapsed. I began to see myself as incurable, which seems to me that I knew my situation was serious but was not willing or did not want to admit it to myself. This was probably through fear of feeling weak, vulnerable and not in control, which is not a space I'm mentally happy to live in, so it was easier to live in denial.

I had to have regular check-ups after my heart attack to check everything was ok but on my next visit for an angiogram all my SATS were all over the place, so my cardiologist was not happy to let me leave the hospital, so a normal hospital visit had resulted in me having to spend another week in hospital. I couldn't believe I was here yet again lying in a ward full of old men. I hated it self-reflection hit me hardest at times like these, as I lay looking at all these older men who have probably led great, active and fulfilling lives who were now hospitalised in their later years as their bodies were giving up on them. Then there's me lying alongside them, a man who was in his younger days, the life and soul of the party, a semi-professional footballer, a strong and dedicated Millwall geezer who had now became a shadow of the man I once was with a body that was giving up on me because I was mentally giving up on myself. As if this wasn't bad enough, when I did get discharged and let home, I returned to find my flat door open and as I walked inside i realised that my flat had been burgled everything had been taken, every electrical item I had was gone, along with my passport and even my dosette boxes of medication. I was absolutely livid that someone was that much of a scummy low life they would even take my tablets! My mum didn't want me to stay at that flat. I don't think it was just the fact that she didn't want me to stay there with no telly or electrical goods but it was also because she knew I was raging and I would end up smashing all my neighbours doors off till I found out who had the audacity to burgle my flat. So I moved back to my mums for a while, which was ok but my drinking still continued although it became harder to hide the severity of the amount I was drinking. I decided to try and self-detox while I was at my mums, and I did this by methods I had learnt at rehabs and addiction classes that I had been to and also learnt by doing my research previously on alcohol abuse to try and understand myself better. I was alcohol dependent so my body could go in to shock and fits by just stopping drinking so a self detox is where over the course of 7-10 days I would lower my alcohol intake daily so my system could slowly get used to the alcohol leaving my body. On day one for example, I would have eight cans, day two I would have seven cans, day three I would have six cans until eventually all the cans got reduced and then I would stop after the last can. I did this a few times and always took myself to my mums to do it, so I wasn't tempted to give in to temptation of having more. I ended up getting another flat in Abbey Wood which was ok with me because it was somewhere of my own and not too far from family and friends. So here I was again trying to give myself yet another fresh start with all good intentions of succeeding but knowing I would fail to beat my demons. Every time I held the upper hand on my life things would start to spiral out of control. I was mentally destroying my state of mind by bombarding my head with depressing thoughts. This would lead me to stop socialising or being around people, therefore feeling alone, then the only comfort I would find would be alcohol and cocaine. It yo-yoed up and down constantly in this same pattern with the drinking and sniffing, getting that bad that my days had no time recognition. I was waking up and as soon as my eyes were open I would reach for a can and down it whole, then I would rack up a line of coke. It didn't matter what time of day it was and to be fair, most of the time I didn't even know what time of day it was. 6am felt the same as 6pm I literally had no concept of time at all and I didn't even care. I had even stopped taking all my medication. I was literally giving up on myself more and more. I was finally realising, after years of denial, I really did have a drink problem because I literally could not stop. I had tried so many times and not stuck to it. So I threw the towel in one day and rang my mum and admitted I needed help. My mum and her partner, Dave, came and picked me up. They helped me pack a bag as they had contacted the rehab I had been in previously and explained how much my mental health was deteriorating due to my heavy addiction. They agreed to section me and put me through another detox. This time I went prepared and even packed my portable DVD player and arrived at 4pm as arranged. I was met at the reception by members of staff who took me to my room which I shared with another guy who had bipolar. He had been in the unit quite a long time and really struggled with his mental health. I was given a course of Librium again as the start of my medical detox. The self-hate that consumed my very existence was on another level, I had let myself deteriorate mentally and physically to now be sitting in a psychiatric unit for the second time and for what....ALCOHOL!!! I hated every inch of myself, i just wanted to escape my own mind and body to run away from every thought that ate away at me, every millisecond reminding me how weak and vulnerable I had allowed myself to become. Every time I spoke to the counsellors they would tell me how intelligent I was and so questioned when enough was enough. The frustrating thing was I knew all the logistics of all the theories and methods of everything they said to me and even put forward conversation that intellectually met them on their own level and psychological structure. Even they couldn't understand why I relapsed so often and bought myself down to such an insignificant level. After five days detox I was feeling a lot better but when I was questioned by the medical staff I was honest and sensible enough to say I didn't feel stable and ready to leave. For me this felt good admitting I wasn't ready; it felt as if I had mentally turned a corner in admittance for my wellbeing. Due to my honest response they agreed I should stay in, which I was happy about. I spoke to my dad who was in bits about me throwing my life down the drain. Looking back I can see how hard it must have been for him., he lived in Spain so didn't really know what was happening in my life as he only knew what I told him on the phone. Coming back to England on a visit, watching his firstborn son who was once a semi-professional footballer, full of life and ambition with so much he could have achieved ahead of him but instead, because of his addiction, he was now visiting a son he didn't recognise anymore wasting his life away. That must have been heart breaking for him! But still he supported me all the way whether he agreed with my life decisions or not. I asked my dad to bring me up some DVDs to watch as on Friday nights we were allowed to order our own food, so I bought everyone pizza which put a smile on lots of peoples faces, especially considering most of them didn't have a support network of people around them to get them things or even had the money to do so. They were even more pleased to see I had a different selection of films to watch so I willingly chose a film to watch in the communal area. I think my choice of DVD was perfect for the environment we was in, my choice being the film "ONE FLEW OVER THE CUCKOOS NEST" I sat watching every ones faces, mesmerized at how similar the story line was to our own situation. I made my excuse to get a drink and left them to enjoy the movie, secretly chuckling to myself on my way out. I found this nearly as funny as their offer of swimming lesson facilities, which I may have taken them up on if it wasn't for the fact they handed me a polystyrene float to do it with. I was feeling a lot better in myself, so when my room-mate went to hospital for the day he lost his bed in the process, and had to go to Woolwich hospital to sleep to then come back her during the day, so I suggested that he had my bed. It was probably the kick up the arse I needed to make me see there are people so much more worse off than myself, who genuinely needed the help. At this point I actually felt like I had cracked it, I was feeling strong and confident enough to face my life outside the unit to try to continue on my own. So the medical staff agreed to ring my mum to pick me up.

Chapter eight

As people sit reading this you can probably feel the frustration on hearing the same repeated pattern I constantly chose to live my life by. With this in mind, can you imagine actually living through this mental torture because I can tell you now it is beyond soul destroying. I never really understood addiction at all and I always associated alcoholism with down and out type characters drinking from brown paper bags. So I basically had a very stereo typical view on the type of people who would fall into this category. That's probably why I lived in denial for so long, never admitting to myself how much my drinking and drug use was totally out of control, even though when I looked in the mirror, staring back at me was the reflection of a person that was unrecognisable to me. This just goes to show everyone this life style is living proof of what addiction does to you. It doesn't matter how strong or weak a person is, as once you fall prisoner to the power of illness it has such a tight hold of you that you become powerless to control any aspect of normality as you know it.

So here I was again, out of rehab for a second time, feeling in control and focused on staying in control now. I got referred to local organisations who deal with drink and drug rehabilitation aftercare as I was adamant on remaining abstinent. Although in the past I never really felt the groups helped me, I thought that it may have been due to the fact I didn't have the right mindset when I attended previously. Also if I was being totally honest I only ever really went before to please everyone else, which is never a good space to come from when you're going through recovery. This time I went with an open mind, ready and wanting all the help I could get. I was feeling determined and stronger now so felt positive that I would maintain it. I chose the classes I wanted to go to and set my days to help me get some sense of structure back. I was assigned a key worker who I spoke to about everything that had happened to me and all I had been through. I even explained to him about my self detoxes that I had done several times before. I did explain to him that if I was being honest with myself I probably did these to convince myself that my drinking wasn't out of control, when my family were throwing their cause for concern at me. In my head I was convinced that if I self detoxed and stopped for a while then I wasn't as dependent on drink as everyone was trying to say I was. My key worker was impressed that I used such knowledge when dealing with my alcoholism. He was however shocked at my tolerance levels to alcohol and said I had the highest he had seen in twenty years of working in his profession. I continued my classes for over two months and was doing really well. I was even considering using all my experience to help others by volunteering to help. Everyone was impressed with the progress I had made. I was even more impressed with myself and really felt like I had turned a corner. One Saturday night I was at home and pre-booked the boxing to watch as George Grove was fighting Carl Froch at Wembley when the phone rang. It was one of my mates asking me where I was watching the fight as a group of them was all meeting up so asked me if I wanted to go? I was hesitant but I wanted to start getting out again, after all I was a bloke and thought I couldn't hide away forever. My mum asked me not to go but I just told her to stop worrying, I was in control now and would only have a couple of Coronas. They're a weak beer and I felt strong enough to be able to socialise on a sensible level and know my limits so I agreed to go and meet them all. This was by far the worst decision I have ever made. I ended up on a four day bender! This time there was no stopping me; it was as if I was making up for the four months I had stopped. What a mug I was, everyone was so annoyed with me. I think they, by now, had accepted the fact that I was always going to be a drinker, whether it killed me or not. They were at the end of the road when it came to trying to help me recover. I was sat in my flat alone when one night I was scrolling through social media and I noticed a girl on there who I had multiple mutual friends with and, by her statuses, I could see she had just come out of a relationship. As I looked through her profile I saw her name was Leanne and she was really pretty so I took my chances and messaged her. She messaged straight back, then we spoke on the phone for ages; it was like we had known each other for ever, we just clicked straight away. We arranged to meet for lunch and I didn't drink at all that day. I realised that I was getting more and more attracted to her the more we spoke and saw each other but I knew deep down I was hiding the shame of my secret alcohol and cocaine use. I kept my drinking to a minimum as we did drink when we was together, like most dating couples do when they're starting a relationship. We hit it off from day one and I really enjoyed every minute we were together which shocked me as I never wanted a relationship, let alone think I'd enjoy being in one. Leanne had her own business so she was busy most days. When she wasn't around I would sit at home drinking and sniffing alone, worried what Leanne would think of me if she could see what a mental mess I was when I was by myself. I introduced Leanne to my family with who she hit it off with straight away. I even got to meet with her kids and absolutely loved feeling part of a family environment and interacting with them all. I even had Leanne and all the kids stay at my flat and looked after them all when she went to work all day. I don't think the kids knew how much I loved spending the day with them. On one of the days we all got up, got ready and jumped in a taxi where we headed off to spend the day up the George Staples pub to watch England play. We all had lunch together; it actually felt so good being out just me and the kids with all my family and loads of mates, who had never seen me with kids around me as I lost any access to my own child. Although not all four of the kids were mine biologically, being there as their dad was the most over whelming feeling I had ever had and I was loving every minute of having them around me introducing them to everyone. Fathers day was coming up and this was another day I always dreaded; a day of the year I would always drink to excess to hide the sorrow that ate away at me each year as it was a reminder of it being another year I hadn't seen my son. This year was different I woke up to a bag of presents and cards Leanne and the kids had got me to show how special they thought I was to them. This gesture meant more to me than they will ever know. This is the first fathers day I had this happen to me and the words Chelsea, Jordane, Shannon and Kye had all written in the cards they gave me were so heart warming and I had never been made to feel like this. I was loving every minute of it and I couldn't believe the impact we had on each other's lives already. Things were slowly starting to look more hopeful for the future. Just having Leanne and the kids in my life now felt like a weight had been lifted off my shoulders and waking up in the morning was becoming easier, knowing my day had a purpose. Although I had so many happy thoughts now going through my head rather than the negativity that had consumed it for so long, there was still a sadness of guilt that weighed heavy in my heart. That was the guilt of my secret life of addiction that Leanne knew nothing about. I do think she had her suspicions as she found some empty cans when she was cleaning up one day. She didn't ask too many questions but she was far from stupid as she was also starting to notice me downing a cans first thing in the mornings. When this happens there is only so many times I could use the excuse that "it was just a quick hair of the dog" or "it was the only drink we had in so I just quickly drank it". The time came for me to be honest and open up, which was really hard for me as I never opened up to anyone before., so I was honest and told Leanne everything. About my drink, the cocaine, rehabs, counsellors, losing contact with my kid, just everything that pushed me into using alcohol as a comfort in my darkest days. I was so glad I told her everything but as I said more and more I was worried incase it pushed her away but it did not one bit. She was very understanding and listened to everything with an open mind and heart and most of all, she never judged me or walked away. Most women I'm sure would have run a mile, but not Leanne, she stood by me and supported me. We started to talk about our future and getting a house together. This was a really big decision as it was not only myself and my position I would have to consider. It would mean us moving areas, kids moving schools and most of all, me really having to be determined to become free of a life I was leading as there was no way I could make all these decisions to be part of Leanne and the kids' lives and be the person I had allowed addiction to turn me into. It would be unfair on everybody and totally selfish of me to put anyone else through the mental turmoil that was my life. But you know what, I had said it so any times before but this time was different. I actually did feel that with the love and support I had from Leanne and the unity I felt being around her and the kids, I honestly did feel I was ready to be able to take a new path and start a new life once and for all. Little did I know that the next path I would be taking was the path of literally fighting for my life!

Chapter nine

It was the end of June and Leanne was with me all day as the kids were at her mums. We had a really good weekend. We were at my brother Paul's house having a get together with him, his missus Kelly, my mum, Dave and sister, all having a wicked time. We were all drinking and the music was playing so everyone was having a dance and generally laughing and joking about till the early hours. Me and Leanne got a taxi home and when we woke up the next day started drinking again. Leanne had a couple then stopped as she knew she had to drive back to her house later because the kids were getting dropped off and she had work the next day. I wasn't feeling that great but didn't think anything of it as I was feeling rough the past few days with stomach pains. I had been coughing and retching then bringing up phlegm with blood in it, but yet again, I didn't think nothing of this either as I had been sniffing cocaine in previous days. Every time I ended up getting on it like I had been I would always end up smoking and as I wasn't a heavy smoker, naturally I just put it down to where I had been smoking more. So yet again I was ignoring warning signals when it came to my health. The day was drawing to an end, so Leanne was getting her bits together to go which straight away put me on a downer as I hated it when she went. It put me back into the lonely space that I had spent so long trying to get away from. I knew she had to go though and had to understand her other commitments. Leanne left hesitantly because she could see I wasn't myself at all and was worried about leaving me alone. As soon as she left I got straight on the phone to call on more gear and made sure I had enough drink for the evening so I could just tuck myself away in my flat. As I lay on the sofa watching telly I leant forward to get my drink and as I did I felt a pain in my stomach. As I did I sat up I just started projectile vomiting repeatedly and where I was sitting in darkness the only light shining into the room was from the telly. As I looked my sick seem to be red. With that vision in my head panic shook through my body as I started fearing for my life so I struggled to my feet as best I could to reach for the light switch to get a better view on what was happening to me. As the light turned on the realisation hit me like a speeding train as all I could see was blood everywhere. I had been vomiting up copious amounts the table and carpet was covered, resembling a scene from a horror movie as all I could see was claret! The next thing I remember was waking up in hospital. I had blood coming out of my mouth and back side. I was completely yellow and my stomach was so swollen I could barely move. Leanne later told me that I had dialled her number when throwing up telling her what was happening then saying, "I'm scared and didn't want to die in my flat alone!" I don't have any recognition of this but it was lucky I did as she rang my mum saying she was worried about me and as she was so far away she couldn't get to me. My mum and Dave came straight to my flat and found me barely conscious and got me rushed to hospital; I don't have any recognition of this either. Leanne said the phone call from me was the scariest phone call she had ever received and she was a bundle of nerves with worry. My mum said walking into my flat that night was one of the worst moments of her life. Looking back I dread to imagine how she felt, bearing in mind that was how we had found her brother when he died. As I lay on the hospital bed fighting for my life the doctors had pulled my mum to one side to warn her I may not make it through the night as, after what I had just been through, I was lucky to have made it to the hospital and was moments from death. As I was laying alone not knowing what the hell was happening, confused and ill like I had never felt before, my whole body hurt from the inside out; my skin was as yellow as Bart Simpson, even the white on my eyeballs was completely yellow. I could hear the doctors talking outside the door and the anxiety set in as they approached to explain my diagnosis, as I knew what I was about to hear wasn't going to be good. Four doctors came in to see me; two stood and two sat down. The fact that they sat down to speak to me rang alarm bells knowing it was bad news. I'd had enough visits to hospital to know that. One of the Consultants began to talk and his first words were, "we've received your notes and test results back from the lab and ultrasound department and it isn't good news!" He went on to explain that I had lost well over two pints of blood and the reason I threw it up was because the ultrasound had confirmed that I had advanced stage four liver Cirrhosis. This meant my liver was not functioning due to the scar tissue and the blood could not get through it. Therefore it pushed the blood outwards up my throat, bursting veins in my oesophagus, causing oesophageal varices which resulted in me having six veins band and glued back together. I hadn't even realised they had done this I just thought my throat was so sore due to vomiting so badly. The doctor said that usually only one or two burst so the fact I burst six and was still alive meant I was a very lucky man. The only words I could string together to ask were the words, "AM I GOING TO DIE?" The doctor's reply was very honest and he said that was down to me. Cirrhosis and oesophageal varices is a very serious illness and also a life threatening disease with an even shorter life expectancy if I didn't make serious changes to my life style. I was in total devastation! My whole world came to a total stand still, it was as if someone had hit the pause button on the world around me as I tried to process exactly what all this meant. As I lay in the ward the hate I felt for myself was beyond immense. All through ignorance, denial and pure selfishness I had allowed addiction to rob me of my life. Although I was actually alive I now only felt like I wasn't living but just existing. I had allowed alcohol to rob me of the person that I was, of my self worth, of my strength, of my pride, of my hopes, of my dreams, of my son, of my respect, of my choices, of anything I wanted to do from this day forward. I literally felt nothing but emptiness.

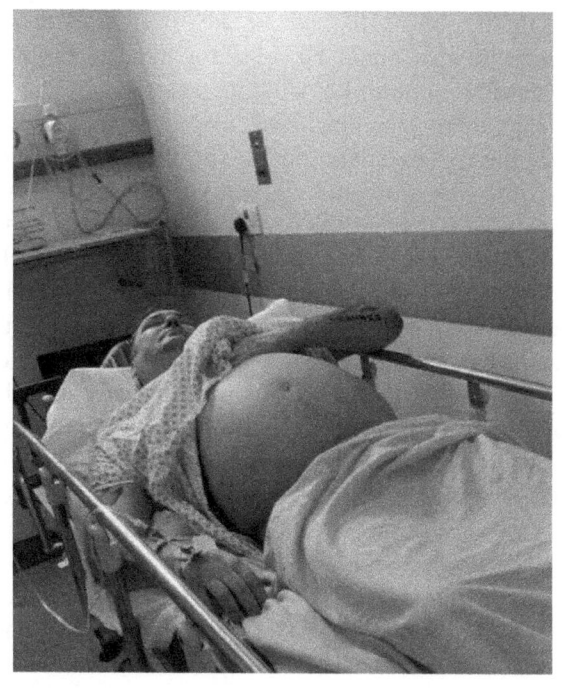

Minutes from death swollen stomach & yellow

Leanne sat with me every day, along with visits from my family and a few friends who were horrified at what I had done to myself. I had now, due to alcohol and cocaine, made myself terminally ill. I had heart disease, advanced liver disease, oesophageal varices and was an insulin dependent diabetic and I was only thirty-nine! As I lay there contemplating my future I looked over to the man laying in the bed beside me; he was exactly the same age as me and after listening to his story, it turns out his life had spiralled out of control exactly the same way mine had. The only difference between us was that he got his diagnosis seven years prior and had relapsed constantly whilst having cirrhosis. There he lay in his bed, literally like a bag of bones, frail as anything and completely yellow. I was watching him staring into space motionless quietly singing to himself the song "going on up to the spirit in the sky." He had already been told there was nothing else that could be done for him, so the hospital were discharging him knowing he was going home to die. As I lay there watching him, knowing he and I were exactly the same age and both given the same diagnosis, I knew from that moment I did not want to leave this earth the same way that guy was, falling prisoner to addiction and dying without one last fight to prove to myself and loved ones that I wanted to live, get my life back and build a future for myself with Leanne and the kids. I made a decision there and then that I would never touch alcohol, cocaine and cigarettes ever again! I was discharged from hospital nine days later with strict guidelines on changes that I had to put into place to make sure my health didn't deteriorate anymore. I was given appointments to be seen by a gastrologists as my oesophagus that had been band and glued needed regular checks as to make sure it didn't re-burst. Also I had to have regular check ups to make sure my liver didn't get worse as it now only had 47% function. Also due to my cirrhosis I would have to have fibro scans and ultra sounds as I would be prone to getting tumours growing. I would have to be under a dietician to have a strict diet to keep my liver functioning properly. The diet they put me on seemed harder than they first realised though as I was an insulin dependent diabetic. which means the diet for diabetes contradicts the diet for cirrhosis which becomes dangerous as that would put pressure on my heart and the stents in my heart so I now needed to see my cardiologist more regularly. My poor doctor was baffled how I would cope because I had now become a medical mystery, as each of my illnesses were serious and potentially life threatening on their own, let alone having all four together! Life at home was hard; I was constantly tired and really struggled to see how I would live my life now. Leanne and my mum did all they could to try and make my life as easy as they could. The tiredness was like torture and all I could see was a life of misery feeling like this. I spoke to my doctor about it who took my blood and realised I had become anaemic. After losing so much blood I ended up having no iron in my body so was taken to hospital again and given two blood infusions. Not long after I began to feel better although life was still tough on a daily basis. I tried my hardest to get on with my life. Leanne and I started looking for our own place together which gave something to look forward to and focus on. My sister, Kelly, told me that she had contacted a guy called Chris Hill who had started up a free addiction session called 'Get Your Life Back', which I was interested to follow through social media, but was not ready to go to, as my recovery was something I wanted to try and do by myself. Everyone kept asking me how I had cirrhosis and whether that meant I would never drink again. What people didn't realise was, yes I did have cirrhosis and one more drink could end my life, but it was still my choice that I didn't drink. Yes, another drink would be dangerous but after my heart attack taking cocaine was also dangerous but I still chose to take it. After I got diabetes and red flags on my liver through alcohol, drinking was dangerous then but I still chose to carry on. So no, I didn't stop because I got cirrhosis, I stopped because it was my choice. cirrhosis just gave me a wakeup call to show me how much I wanted to stay alive. I knew my journey was going to be hard, even as determined as I was, because once you're addicted you remain an addict for the rest of your life; it's just whether you're strong enough to not feed your addiction anymore. I spoke to Leanne and she agreed to take me to Chris Hill's workshop and everyone there had different problems and his group was like no other I went to, people's problems ranged from alcoholism, drug abuse, food addiction, gambling, smoking and anxiety. Chris worked on retraining your mind to help people in all areas of life. I found his technique really good and it really opened my mind. Once Chris knew my story, he was totally gob smacked at everything I had been through and was still alive to tell the tale; he also found my knowledge of alcoholism and drug use fascinating. We arranged to meet in a coffee shop a few days later and asked me if I would mind sharing my story to help inspire others and also my journey would help spread the dangers that addiction could cause to your health. His jaw nearly hit the floor when I showed him my dosette boxes where I needed to take 904 tablets a month now to stay alive. I agreed to help out and was glad that I could maybe now turn all the negative things that I had been through into something positive to help others. The first talk I did was in Bloomsbury square, London and it was in front of about one hundred people and to say I was nervous was an understatement. Don't get me wrong, I am a naturally confident bloke but this is something I had never done before and was so much out if my comfort zone. I was as nervous as anything and Leanne was by my side all day giving me all the support she could and filled me full of confidence, so when I got up to speak I didn't hold back. I told them all my story from the start, being a semi-professional footballer all the way through to how I deteriorated more and more through battling with addiction. It actually felt good sharing my story. Years ago I would never have stood there in front of all of those people and I would never have had the courage to admit how weak I had allowed my addiction to make me and especially talking out loud sober as well. I could tell by the audience's reaction that I really did touch people and hit home with a lot of them and if I'm being honest, the people still sitting there who were still drinking and using drugs were actually scared by what they heard me say. I don't think people actually realise the danger they put themselves in being alcohol dependent. I mean everyone knows what cirrhosis, oesophageal varices, diabetes and heart disease are, not many people know anyone who has all four of these life- threatening Illnesses, or have lived through having them to be able to show others it has affected their lives. So I actually felt good that, although I never helped myself, soon enough I may be able to help someone else, and that really did feel good. When the seminar had finished I was so pleased I had stuck it through and listened to Leanne and drew strength from helping others. It was so rewarding and a better feeling than I got from any drink or drug. I was really starting to feel good about staying sober, and although my health had dramatically deteriorated, I was starting to look forward to the future. Leanne spent every spare moment she could with me so when we finally got a moving in date for a new place together we were both totally over the moon. Everything was finally falling into place for us. In October I had my 40th birthday which for most people was a big celebration, but for me it was also a milestone, as I honestly in my darker days never saw me ever reaching forty, yet here I was with a family and close friends not only celebrating but doing it sober and it felt good. I'd be lying if I said I found it easy being out with everyone celebrating and watching them still drinking around me because it wasn't, it was really challenging. However I did it since I gave up every addiction I had; Leanne did the same too, not that she had to because she didn't. She did it out of pure love and support for me. I honestly don't think I could have done it without her. Christmas and New Year came and went. It was hard as I didn't get to spend it with Leanne as her dad was critically ill so her and the kids spent it with her mum and dad as it would be ther last Christmas with him. They did ask me to come too but I didn't; not because I didn't want to, but because I obviously struggle with the side effects of my illnesses on a daily basis and I didn't want Leanne to be worrying about me as it was important that she spent as much time with her dad while she still could. When our moving date came in February it was like having all our Christmases come at once. On the day of moving I'd like to say I was there grafting but I wasn't. Instead I had my first Millwall game out with my mates sober and without cocaine. My friends were really supportive and picked me up and dropped me home because it would be too tiring for me to get public transport and they even offered not to drink while I was there. I told them to all drink and carry on as normal; I didn't want to be a drain on people. This was my illness and everyone else didn't need to put their lives on hold to accommodate me. I felt bad enough I couldn't help Leanne move but she totally understood that I'd feel useless not being able to lift or do anything strenuous as advised by my doctors; she even encouraged me to go to Millwall for the day. As we started settling in to family life together things were really going well. We were still going to Chris Hill's workshop regularly, which did help me stay focused. I then got a letter from my cardiologist giving me a date in May for my appointment at St Thomas to check the stability of my heart after my cirrhosis diagnosis. First of all I had to have an endoscopy which is a camera put down my throat to check the varices on my oesophagus, as any procedures I now have done on my heart would make me more high risk in case the veins I had band and glued re-burst. We were really enjoying settling into family life together. I thought things would be hard at first especially given the fact that two of Leanne's kids were teenagers but we all really got on from day one and I was loving every minute of family life with me Leanne and all four kids.

Millwall west block upper crew 19 months sober

Bad news fell on us though in the April as I heard one of my life-long best mates, Danny Goddard, had been told he was terminally ill with cancer and there was nothing more that could be done for him. When me, Leanne and my mum went to see him my heart broke into pieces. Dan was a massive part of my life growing up and always one of the boys, but when I saw him, brain surgery had left him unable to speak properly and he hated us seeing him like it. You know what, I didn't think of him as any different to me. He was still good old Dan. I was gutted beyond belief that this would be the last time I would see him and he sadly passed away three weeks later. He was only forty-one with a lovely missus, Lou, and a beautiful young daughter, Erin. This was the first major event that happened to me whilst being sober and yes, the first thing I wanted to do was hit the bottle and drink myself through the pain of losing my friend but I didn't. Leanne was there with me every step of the way, showing me that I didn't need to drink to deal with grief; reminding me that the more I dealt with sober the stronger it would make me, mentally and emotionally. I kept this in my mind and with Leanne's love and support I stayed sober and didn't pick up a single drink. Then, a couple of weeks later we had more bad news, Leanne's dad sadly passed away after losing his battle with cancer too. How Leanne coped, I'll never know. Not only was she dealing with her own pain but also the pain of the four children too who were devastated losing their granddad and all the same time looking after me and supporting me. So we then had three really hard days. On Monday I had my appointment at St Thomas where I had a stress echo on my heart. Where they found more problems which meant I would need coronary artery intervention. This news was hard to take as I knew this procedure was more complicated and because of my other illnesses, I was now high risk as well, so panic set in. Leanne kept me strong, reminding me of how far I'd come and whatever happened she would be by my side. Then on the Tuesday it was Danny's funeral. The day was so hard, watching the pain his family were going though losing him so young, it was devastating. As I watch them speaking and crying I couldn't help but think this could have easily been my funeral and my family going through this months earlier. This opened my eyes up to how differently things could have turned out for me. This left me reminiscing on how selfishly I had led my life, destroying my health through my addiction and here we were burring Danny when he had no choice over his illness that took his life from him! Then on the Wednesday it was Leanne's dad's funeral. I didn't go to this with her as, although on the outside I looked like I was healthy and fine, the truth behind closed doors was that I was very ill and had two really hard days and was struggling to keep my strength up. Leanne totally understood how I felt and said that she would rather me look after myself first. I did feel absolutely gutted that Leanne was always there for me and caring for me on a daily basis, yet here I was on a day when she probably needed me more than ever, not being able to be there for her. This was yet another kick in the teeth; as it was a reminder that due to what I had allowed addiction do to me, I now had choices like these taken out of my hands enabling me not to be physically able to do the things I needed to do! Yet again Leanne put her feelings to one side and put my feelings and well-being before her own, fully supporting me even after this week, being the hardest three days ever. These are all situations that I would never have been able to cope with, without alcohol but I did! Even as hard as it was, with the love, support and strength I had gained by having a strong woman by my side I get through it all. It was moments like these that made me realise I had met my soul mate and for the first time in my life, I had met a woman who I loved like I had never loved someone before and really did want to spend the rest of my life with. I took Leanne to Denny's seafood restaurant where I proposed and she said yes to becoming my wife, making me the happiest man alive. We booked the wedding straightaway.

Me with Leanne & kids after heart surgery

Life with all these illnesses has its good and bad days as there are so many side effects to cirrhosis that people don't realise; one being not being able to sleep which did get me down a lot as it left me feeling constantly tired and aching, making my life hard. We tried to keep life as normal as possible as so many changes were made to help me stay sober and appreciate other things in life that I had missed out on through addiction. We got season tickets for

Millwall for myself, Leanne and Kye, who is only seven, so we could have days out together. There was a method in my madness buying Leanne hers as she drives so she could come every match with me, so if i started struggling and feeling ill, she can bring me home so I'm not a burden on my mates. Also Kye loves football so we finally started to be able to get out a bit more. It was mental going to Millwall with my missus and boy as I had always only gone with my mates but loved every minute of it. July came and I got to celebrate my first year being sober. I was absolutely buzzing and so proud of myself. Never in a million years did I ever see myself being a whole year clean of all addictions. I had reached my first milestone of many to come. My due date for my heart operation came up and I'm not afraid to admit it but I was scared. Although I had heart work done already this was my first lot done after being diagnosed with cirrhosis and oesophageal varices. I was a wreck for days with worry but Leanne was by my side every minute being my rock and giving me strength to face it, which I did. Two hours in surgery and I was told I needed more work done on the back of my heart and I was proud of how well I coped. The longer I was staying sober the stronger I was feeling, mentally and emotionally. I had so much being thrown at me and never once did I give in to addiction for support. It was this good feeling I got that made me decide I wanted to help others more so I spoke to Leanne about it and she gave her full support, as always and together we started a social media page support group to help people struggling with alcohol addiction. We promoted it everywhere we could so people knew we were here to help, listen and support them and their families should they want to get free of the demon that is alcohol and more often than not cocaine. We were amazed that so many people wanted to know my story and could relate to it and use what happened to me as an inspiration to stop. Leanne then went one step further and designed us a web page called www.yourchoice-alcohol.co.uk. bless her, she has never done anything like that before in her life, but she researched how to do it and spent the next week making it happen. She did amazing. The web page shares my story, shows the dangers of addiction, shows videos her and my mum made so family members of addicts can see they're not alone and we provided contact details so people can come to us for help. We also set the home detox programme I used to show other people how to withdraw from alcohol safely, and not put themselves at risk when choosing to become sober. People started to make contact with us but all conversations were confidential; we would speak to them about their addictions, problems they were having and changes they wanted to make in their lives. Leanne and I made sure we stayed in contact with them daily as I knew from personal experience how important a support network was whilst in recovery. There were also people who were alcohol dependent and so needed to go through a detox programme and these had been turned away by doctors and given Valium to help them until they could be seen by other recovery classes. So we met with the people who needed a detox and showed them the programme I used and made ourselves available 24hrs a day and with our help, a number of people have already got clean and stayed sober. Once we helped them, be that with a detox or not, we would then introduce them to Chris Hill so he could help them as well with their after-care, by re training their minds to help maintain their recovery. The more people that came to us the more people we introduced to Chris, bearing in mind our web page had over 6,000 views in less than five months, so there were quite a few. Chris took us both with him to give a talk to a pre-rehab group where I shared my story and I think, letting people who were vulnerable and desperate like I was only twenty months before, gave some of these people hope as I was once in their shoes and so they could feel I understood and wasn't sitting there talking about addiction from a text book perspective but from a living proof perspective. Which believe me, this makes such a difference to somebody looking for answers and a way out, like those people were. When we left we handed out our business cards we got printed up so people knew they could contact us if they wanted or needed to at any point, which they did, as sometimes all some ones needs to hear is a voice that understands and never judges them, which we don't and never would. Chris also took us with him to a book signing with Russell Brand. We went and met his dad Ron Brand and Brandon Block first. Two lovely blokes. Then we went straight to the signing. I never in a million years thought I would be standing chatting to Russell Brand, especially given the fact he is a West Ham fan! But he was a lovely bloke and we shared stories about our recovery, just proving even more that it doesn't matter what walk of life you're from, addiction can get hold of anybody at any time. This made me even more determined to want to spread the awareness as much as I could. Even when I had my next lot of heart surgery, which was really high risk due to the main oxygen supply at the back of my heart getting worked on, even though I was so nervous and even worried I wouldn't make it through the procedure, I still tried to use my experience by keeping a daily video diary to show people how much I struggle on a daily basis and having to have Leanne now care for me, to show people the dangers of alcohol and cocaine addiction to spread the awareness as much as I could. People who I had known all my life had never actually seen how much I struggled behind closed doors.

Me and Leanne with Russell Brand

Chapter ten

I found using my experience of my own addiction to help others really helped give me a new focus and a new meaning to life. For me, it felt like I had spent so many years full of negative energy that consumed every inch of me, fuelling my reasoning behind why I used alcohol and cocaine as a coping technique. Yet here I was physically at the worst stage of my life feeling nothing but positivity to why this had happened to me. I could have quite easily been angry at the fact that I was now living with four chronic illnesses and rebelled as I always did and thought 'I've messed my life up fully now so fuck it, I'm gonna go out with a bang!' But I didn't. Instead I turned everything that should have destroyed me into a positive and told myself 'This happened to me for a reason and it's only right that I should use my story to show others how easily addiction can destroy your life, relationships, mental health and also the medical damage it can cause!' I felt that with me having the status I did around so many of my connected areas I could be the one person that people look at and think 'If Rodney stone can do it, anyone can!' and it worked. The minute people saw me, a 6 foot 2 inches geezer, ex-hooligan, ex-semi-professional footballer, ex-thug, who once wanted to fight the world who now turned my life around completely and want to help others suffering like I once was and tell them my journey from start to finish, it really opened their eyes and minds to give them hope that there is a way out of the dark hole they were living in. The shock factor people get when I show them my weekly dosette box full of 1,268 tablets for the month that I have to now take to stay alive, all because of alcohol and cocaine is immense and a real eye opener for addicts. Don't get me wrong, I still have my down days where I self-hate. Like for example when I had my stag do. My best mate Scott arranged it, but I had to stay fairly close to home just incase I came over ill and needed to be collected by Leanne quickly. All week prior to it I knew it would hard, bearing in mind there was forty-five blokes all drinking, with the majority of them all still doing cocaine. The thought of going and being the centre of attention but not being able to still be the life and soul of the party, the not-give-a*fuck type geezer I once was, joining in the drinking and cocaine fuelled after parties that often ended up happening, filled me full of anxiety through the roof. But I faced it and joined in all the laughs, reminiscing and socialising with all my family and mates, watching them all get smashed out of their heads, enjoying themselves and I remained sober. Every one of them there had nothing but respect and admiration for me and it felt good knowing that not any of them for one moment thought any less of me and still saw me for who I was now. It was not till I got home that the self-hate hit me a bit, but it was more that I was angry at myself for putting myself in a position medically that I had, all because I ignored all the warning signs and just carried on living life thinking I was indestructible. I was now living my life with no choices, through my own arrogance! When I feel like this I can now quickly snap myself out of it by reinforcing all the positive things I have in my life now. I think one of the main concerns people have when wanting to stop drinking or any other addiction, is how they will still socialise or interact with friends who will still be living the life style that they are trying to leave behind. This is something I was always scared about and probably, if I'm being honest, was most of the reason I relapsed so many times. I wouldn't begin to try and insult anyones intelligence by saying it was easy because it's not. It actually takes a really strong mind and a great positive mental attitude to make a life changing decision to choose and stick to better life choices. I would strongly suggest to anyone facing these changes to set some sort of plan in action to stop them from relapsing too.

Stag do boys

I would firstly suggest you be honest with friends and family who you drink or use drugs with by letting them know what changes you're making to your life style and also be honest about why you are choosing to do so. I have learnt that those people who genuinely care about you and your welfare do support any positive decisions in your life you choose to make. Then those that are not supportive may need to stay out of the equation until you are strong enough to know that their opinion is insignificant to your life. When you are at the beginning of your journey I would strongly suggest also that you pick what social events you need to be part of wisely, only because at the beginning of any freedom journey your mind control can so easily switch. You may start off feeling good about stopping and be overly confident that there's no turning back. Then, for example, the moment you are in an environment where everyone is drinking and letting their hair down, more often than not making calls ordering cocaine or smoking like it's going out of fashion, your mind will start trying to convince you of thoughts like

'You don't need to stay clean!' or 'One more drink won't hurt!' Then the anxiety sets in, making your self-control weaken, no matter how much you don't want to use again. So socialising is still possible but pick wisely where you choose to be and who you choose to be with, just until your mind is fully prepared for every situation you may face. People will be shocked to realise how many times there are triggers for an addiction. For example, if we look at cocaine use, most people who I have helped, confided in me for advice and even from my own experiences, say they only use cocaine when they drink, or only smoke when they have a drink or use drugs. Some people will say they only drink when they are in certain situations or environments. That's when people need to address the fact that there are triggers for each addiction. So for instance, people know as soon as they have a drink the brain will TRIGGER a WANT for cocaine, the brain will TRIGGER a WANT for cigarettes. Others know as soon as they are with certain people or in certain environments the brain will TRIGGER a WANT for a drink because it identifies only being able to deal with any of the three things with alcohol. So the core problem can only be resolved by getting to the root of what causes it. People may only think they have a cocaine problem that is an addiction out of control, so they still want to socialise and go out drinking but want to stop the WANT for cocaine. Yet when people come face to face with the reality that they only use it after consuming alcohol, they can see that the moment they cut out the trigger for their addiction i.e. being aware of their alcohol intake, they can begin to free themselves of the want for cocaine. We have worked with people who have cut out drinking to stop their WANT for cocaine and once they feel free of the need to participate in the consumption of it they then start to socialise as they did before and start drinking again, but this time they felt able to say no to the TRIGGER in their mind that once appeared every time they drank. Lots of people think I am anti-drink or anti-drugs which could not be more further from the truth as I am not anti either of these things. I am the first to admit I had some of the best times of my life of both. What I am is anti-any addiction that controls your life, mind and ultimately your health as it did mine. People going through recovery also need to be honest with themselves and dig deep and try to deal with what makes them feed their addictions. One of my first TRIGGERS that fed mine was not being able to have contact with my first born son. So every time I drank I would get more angry at the situation then my mind would be over loaded with thoughts, scenarios, the what ifs, the but whys? The more I thought about it the more annoyed I would get then the more I drank, till in the end it ate away at me every day. Until ultimately it controlled my everyday life TRIGGERING my addiction. What I try and encourage people to do is try to mentally and emotionally deal with the core problem that made them become an addict. As I found no matter how much you want freedom from an addiction if you are drinking to deal with mental trauma, unless you find peace within your mind to be able to close the door on the situation that is controlling your addiction in the first place the want and the need to mask it will always be there. Yes you may still be angry or emotionally scarred but you need to be able to draw strength from the fact that 'yes you let that situation break you, but you also let it make you better, to be able to build yourself up into a much stronger person!' Addiction will be the hardest battle you ever have to face and is a life long illness that will always be there. I strongly believe I will always be an addict I just choose not to feed my addiction anymore. If you can beat addiction you can beat anything life throws at you.

Before I become sober I never would have dreamt that I would be sitting with NHS staff at Oxleas telling them my journey and being put forward with Leanne to become a Lived Experience Volunteer Practitioner. Even staff with many years of experience working with vulnerable people who are in the position I once was were shocked at the life style I led and how young I was to have suffered the illnesses I had. They were however grateful that I was sat there telling them that I wanted to help others before it was too late for them to recover. The fact that I had become so ill due to addiction and although I still struggle everyday myself, i still wanted to help others who were struggling and this was very rare for them to see. It was at these meetings I got asked to work at local rehab clinics sharing my journey to help inspire others. I could never put fully into words the over whelming joy I felt walking into the rehab wards where I had once been admitted to, wearing my NHS badge sitting on the opposite side of the table looking face to face with people in desperate need of hope, to know that there is a way out of the dark hole that they felt their life was in right then. I could almost see a glimpse of hope light up in their eyes when I told them that only 2yrs prior to that day I was sitting where they were now. For them to know that I was once drink and drug dependent,vulnerable, scared, lonely depressed and every other emotion that they were feeling at that very moment spoke volumes. To be as low as they were and for them to know at that point that at least one person knew exactly how they were feeling gave them some hope and for me to give somebody hope at that stage of their life gave me hope that I may have made a difference to somebody else's life. I would encourage anybody who has been through addiction and beat it to always share their story as so many people feel alone and like no-one understands how they're feeling or what they are going through. Although people who work with vulnerable people do an amazing job they will never be able to reach an addict on a compassionate level to understand how their brain works, as no text book learning can help you reach out to them to know what they truly need to know in terms of how to help. This is one of the main reasons that although we were working with the NHS and Oxleas when my good friend Chris Hill said he wanted to open a shop to help people with addiction and life style changes and needed help with alcohol advice, I jumped on board with that too. Chris already run workshops to help people get their life back and was able to help with a lot of addictions as he too had been free of drink and drugs for over 8 years and lost his identical twin brother through Ecstasy 4 years prior. However he didn't have an understanding on what an alcoholic goes through on a daily basis as alcohol addiction is a totally different ball game and so easily available when it comes to addiction. I set in place with Chris that if anyone came into the shop or his work shop who was struggling with alcohol i would deal with them first of all, as like I mentioned previously they would find it easier opening up to somebody who has walked in their shoes. So what I do is meet with the person first of all, in a destination of their choice, as it is important to be in an environment that they find comfortable enough to be able to open up and talk. I always start by introducing myself and tell them a bit about why I do what I do so they can see why I am passionate about it, plus it also shows them that I mean what I say when I promise them that I will not judge anything that they confide in me about. This is important when you try and support people as all addicts feel judged on their addiction which gives them the perception that no one will understand. I also find that by me saying about my journey first it builds an immediate sense of trust for them to be honest about what they're going through, why they are going through it and most importantly, being honest about their level of alcohol consumption. Once I know these major factors I can then set them their own personal reducing detox programme. As anyone knows if you are drinking everyday it can be dangerous to stop immediately so the reduction detox not only prepares your mind for gradually becoming abstinent but it also prepares your body for the withdrawal without it being a shock to the system. I like to set the programmes for between seven to fourteen days, all depending on the volume and amount a person is drinking. With spirits as the volume is too high and the drinks cannot be measured properly and often than not gets drunk too quickly, I never put anyone on a top shelf detox. I always suggest Ciders, Lagers or even Wine, which ever is their preferred choice. If they are top shelf drinkers and i am changing their drink I would have to work out the amount and volume of the drink they are consuming and set the detox to a lower volume but on a same daily volume intake, or as close as I can so their body can go into withdrawal properly. For example:

1litre of Vodka = 37.5%vol = 33 shots or 15 doubles so If they chose wine as their preferred drink I would suggest it be the 14% vol and I would set their detox programme like this:

NUMBER OF DAYS	ALCOHOL INTAKE
DAY 1:	8 glasses
DAY 2:	7 glasses
DAY 3:	6 glasses
DAY 4:	5 glasses
DAY 5:	5 glasses
DAY 6:	4 glasses
DAY 7:	3 glasses
DAY 8:	2 glasses
DAY 9:	2 glasses
DAY 10:	1 glass

I would also suggest to people to get as much support as they can through the withdrawal process. Where possible It helps to only have the set amount you should have for the day in the house and I would also ask for them if they do struggle with temptation, to not have access to extra money whilst going through the programme so then there is no temptation to exceed your daily limit. This may seem drastic but it is essential as the anxiety can sometimes be too hard to deal with and anxiety is all part of the withdrawal process and completely normal. To help deal with the anxiety I do advise people to set themselves goals for the things they want to achieve and hope to do once sober, as life becomes so much clearer and to create change you need a purpose so you have a reason to face each day as you will no longer be masking your days with alcohol. I also make sure that anyone detoxing from drink or drugs always sees their GP to get checked over to make sure they are medically fit and no damage has been done. Blood tests will check all major organs, blood sugars and generally make sure your health is not at risk. For people who come through the shop who don't have support I will offer to go to them and even budget their drink and visit them daily. For anyone who wants freedom from alcohol and wants to follow a detox programme like I have set but do not have a support network of any kind or help daily but really do need help as you cannot function without alcohol, I would strongly advise that you go to a hospital to tell them how much you are struggling and asked to be referred to a detox centre. That way you may get the help you need with 24 hour support and a medical detox treatment. The withdrawal process is more intense and done through medication called Librium (which is a medication that give your body the same feeling as alcohol) so you do have to be mentally strong to prepare yourself first. I myself as you have already read in previous chapters, went to the hospital and detox centres many times but always relapsed. If I am being totally honest that was due to my own ignorance by not continuing the help services that are available for people with addiction and these groups have helped many friends and people I know. I think at the time of my rehab stays I was doing the detox for everyone else's peace of mind that I was trying to get clean rather than for the want of wanting to help myself as I didn't believe I was as bad as I actually was. So when I saw the people that attended the addiction services I would put myself in a different league to convince myself I didn't need to be there, so not to be tarred with the same brush as the people that already attended them. Looking back in hindsight now that was a very bad judgement on my behalf because if I hadn't have been so ignorant and judgemental I could have realised sooner that I needed help just as much, if not more, than all of the people I thought I was better than. For those reasons shown when choosing to become clean you really do have to do it because it is what YOU AND ONLY YOU WANT! As this is the only way you will make it happen. It has taken me years of fighting demons that caused not only addiction but also anxiety, depression, solitude, loneliness and more often than not, times of wanting to end my life where I literally saw no way out of the hole I had become buried in, to then become minutes from dying for me to wake up and realise that I have so much more to my life and worth living for. I refused to allow myself to become another statistic on the already rising number of victims that were losing their battle against addiction. It takes a lot to reach the moment that you want to change your life. I now find happiness in places I never knew existed for people like me but through all these achievements my greatest to date was the day I finally married the love of my life. The one woman who stood by me through everything, the good days, the bad days, and more often than not, the very ugly days. She is more than just my partner, she really is my soul mate and best friend and on June 2nd 2018 she was officially my wife. I was an emotional wreck watching her being walked up the aisle by our son Kye. She looked more beautiful than ever, tears of happiness rolled down my face; it was as if every emotion that I had blocked out for years came back rushing through my body. As we exchanged our vows I listened smiling from ear to ear as Leanne agreed to be mine till death us do part and at that moment I became the happiest man on the planet. I had never felt love like I felt for Leanne. She literally saved my life and I owe her everything as she saw nothing but good in me when I had nothing but hate for myself. It was when I sat in our wedding reception filled with a room full of at least 150-180 people, who were all family and friends and all of them gleaming with happiness at being able to share our wedding day. So many of them there honestly believed at stages of my life that they would all only be together like this for my funeral rather than my wedding. The over whelming sense of pure happiness, contentment and sheer pride that I felt for myself for the life I was now living was the best feeling in the world. My life had literally come full circle and excelled in ways I could only have ever dreamt of; if only I could sell bottles of how good this feeling was the world would be an amazing place for everyone. It was because of these feelings that I now felt every day that I wrote this book in the hope that I could share my story to help others see that they are not alone. My struggle will always continue behind closed doors with my health but my journey will go on to a positive path in the future. As this book comes to an end I hope everyone reading it has realised just how quickly a weekend binge drinking and cocaine session can easily get out of control and can so easily be detrimental to your health. My journey to freedom from addiction is something I never thought possible let alone achievable but here I am, living proof that anything is possible but it has got to be....YOUR CHOICE

Me, Leanne and both Mums

Wedding ceremony guests

THE OUTSIDE IN

by Leanne Stone

When I first met Rodney I never thought for one minute our life would take us on the journey it has, but I'm a strong believer that everything happens for a reason and considering how many times we should have met in the past, especially considering we grew up in the same area and knew the same circles of friends our paths never crossed but did at the right time.

As soon as we started talking we connected straight away. We were on the phone for ages and his personality was larger than life. I spent more time laughing than talking and that's one thing that has always shone through about him since that day, no matter what life threw at him he still always managed to find something to laugh about. We met for the first time at a shopping centre and looking back I always laugh because most girls would have probably run a mile. As we started off walking about, talking and laughing then after about ten minutes I wanted to look in a few shops because it was nearly my daughter's birthday. As soon as I started looking at trainers Rod starting getting stressed, walking in and out the shop, telling me "he would leave me there if I didn't hurry up" then it was me telling him "to piss off then!" We were in the shop, with people staring at us like we were a married couple having a domestic, laughing at us as he stormed off telling me "he'd wait for me in the pub!" So I just continued what I was doing then walked to the pub where he was drinking a beer. We then sorted out our differences the way we always do, even now, and that's to take the mickey out of each other, then laugh it off. I mean who meets each other for the 1st time after only talking on the phone and ends up in situations like that? I think it was due to the fact that from the first minute we spoke we instantly clicked and it was like we had known each other for years and been together forever. I never really noticed that Rod had a drink problem and can honestly say I never saw him drunk and considering knowing now how much he was actually drinking it seems obscured. It's not until I look back at moments in our past that make sense now I know he had a problem, that his drinking pattern was not right, . Like having to go into a pub even on a shopping trip. In the beginning though there were no triggers for alarm because I always only considered we were doing what every other couples our age was doing and that was meeting up. If we weren't going out, which we often didn't as we didn't need to be round people we had so many good times just in each others company, we would just go to the shop where he would get his ciders and he would get me a couple of bottles of wine. Obviously I knew he was doing cocaine but i didn't know the extent of the damage he had done to his heart already and we were growing up in an era where EVERYBODY I knew did cocaine or other drugs. In fact you would find it hard to find somebody in our day and age that didn't participate in doing cocaine and drinking and more often than not, not just at weekends either. So I had no reason to find it strange that he was doing it and he did it before we met, so the way I saw it was that it needed to be his decision not to do it rather than try and change him. The first time I remember thinking he may have a drink problem was when I found half empty cider bottles in his cupboard at his flat when I was tiding up and when I picked them up and asked him why they were in there, his whole face changed and for the first time I saw him annoyed at me. Obviously looking back I now know he wasn't angry at me, he was angry at the fact that I had caught him hiding a drink problem he wasn't ready to admit to having. He tried to quickly back out of the conversation by playing it down and saying he put it in there because he didn't want to admit he was drinking that day as we had plans and the way he reacted to it I could see he was uncomfortable talking about it so I didn't push him any further about the situation. It wasn't long though before I did have to start addressing his drinking habits with him because I started to notice him downing a can first thing in the morning. First of all he did try to use all the usual excuses that an alcohol addict would probably come out with, things like "I just needed a drink and that's all there was to have!" or "I'm just having one to straighten my head out!" so I had to say to him I think you have a problem. to which he would try and shrug off by saying "don't be stupid, when have you ever seen me lagging?" and in defence he was right because I hadn't., yet on the flipside of that quote, knowing what I know now about his drinking addiction, the truth was although I may have never seen him lagging the reality was I actually had never seen him fully sober! I never went mad and pushed him into stopping drinking all together, this is because Rod is a very strong man's man type of character who wouldn't be told to do anything he didn't want to do so I knew if I demanded he stopped I would have just pushed him away and he would have drank more. So as he always insisted he never had a drink problem what I did was try to make him test himself to see if he was alcohol dependent. I did this by asking (not telling him) to not drink first thing in the morning, so as he was insistent he 'didn't need' his drink in the morning I would say, "ok if you don't need to drink, try not to have it first thing in the morning and maybe wait till lunchtime?" Give him his due he did try to do this but he found it hard. I noticed that after being awake about an hour he would start to get twitchy and try every excuse to try and have that first beer. So I would not make a big fuss, I would make a joke and say, "come on you're nearly there, just wait till lunchtime. You're only drinking out of habit! Just try to prove to yourself you don't ACTUALLY need it." He found it hard at first and starting only getting till about 10am before he had a can, but he did start getting nearly to lunchtime. I really can say I felt we were getting somewhere, and finally maybe finding a solution to his addiction but unfortunately it was all too late as the decision whether he could choose to drink or not got taken out of our hands. It was July 1st 2016. After having an amazing few days spending quality time with the kids, spending time with Rods family and going to a family party, I had to leave Rod at his flat and didn't spend the night with him, which we both hated because we hated being apart from each other. So on the nights we weren't together we would be on the phone continuously and on this night inhparticular I didn't want to leave him, because he hadn't been himself and had been coughing up bits of blood in his phlegm for over a week. I had also noticed he kept on blacking out without realising so I was begging him to go the doctors but he hadn't yet been. So I made sure I kept him on the phone line, even if he was on speaker while I was still pottering around doing what I needed to do. It had got quite late and he said he wasn't feeling well and he had to go because he was going to be sick. I waited for him to ring back but he didn't so I kept ringing. My hands were trembling more and more every time I couldn't get through, so when he finally answered I could hear from his trembling voice he was terrified. My heart was sinking as he was saying he was being sick and there was blood in it. I'll never forget the sound of his voice saying " I'm scared babe, I don't want to die in this flat on my own!" Those words still bring a tear to my eye every time I think about that night, when I was at the end of a phone feeling helpless, being so far away knowing I couldn't get to him and not knowing what to do for the best. So I did no more than ring his mum telling her I was really worried about him and told her what was happening and I couldn't get to him because I was so far away and all the kids were asleep. She told me not to worry and she would go straight to his flat and ring me when she knew what was happening. For the rest of that night the minutes seemed like hours, the hours seemed to pass like years before I heard from his mum. It was without a doubt the longest night of my life. When I spoke to his mum her voice sounded so drained and exhausted as she told me it wasn't good news; he had thrown up loads of blood, he was yellow with jaundice and was really weak so I told her I was on my way to the hospital. When I got there my heart fell through my stomach as I looked at my big, strong fearless man looking so ill, vulnerable and weak. For the first time I could see in his eyes he was scared but we all were, I was obviously thanking god endlessly that he was still here with us because of how close he was to losing his life just hours before but so many thoughts were flooding into my head as I watched him lying there just like a broken shell of the man that he was the day before. Some of the questions that came with the guilt were things like, 'should I have done something sooner?' 'Should I have never drunk with him when we were drinking in doors as it might have made him stop?' 'Should I have stayed with him that night instead of going home?' 'Should I have stayed with him every day until we got on top of his drinking problem so I knew he would be ok to be left on his own and not drink?' 'Should I have dealt with it better and been harder on him and not been afraid of pushing him away so he was made to stop sooner?' but looking back, Rod was so strong minded that in reality the truth is, would he of actually listened to any of the doubts and guilt that I carried to have made things any different to how they were? It's then that I had to deal for the first time with knowing he had now made himself terminally ill, with a life threatening illness so I didn't know if he could even ever get better? How long he had to live? What would life be like now he was this close to dying? How would it not only affect Rod but also me and our children who idolise him; how would they deal with this? What quality of life would we all have now? Not only all of us individually but for us all as a family unit? Would we be able to cope? How would we cope? The questions that raced through my brain were endless. The more questions that popped into my head the more the weight of the world fell upon my shoulders, but no matter what question came up, not once did I ever question that I would never not be by his side every step of the way. My shoulders were broad and I knew I had to be strong enough to get Rod, myself and our children through this as they all needed me more now than ever.

FROM A FRIEND'S VIEW

Danny Callaghan

Right, where do I start! My name is Danny Callaghan. Rodney has been a very, very good friend of mine, he's been one of my best pals for nearly twenty-five years now. If I told you some of the things we used to get up to you would think I was talking out of my arse! Many occasions we've been out on two or three day benders with plenty of booze which led to plenty of tear-ups. Remembering on occasions myself, Rodders and our other pal, Scott Beddows had been Millwall (Carlisle) and the boozing started off at 10:00 in the morning, the boozing then the other bits and pieces came out, we ended up in a pub in Crayford fucking lagging. When it came to closing time none of us could talk, let alone try and get home. It was absolutely pissing down so we walked to the cab office but there were no cabs. I think we were in such a state that no cunt wanted to take us! We ended up sitting at the bus stop for fuck knows how long. Rod had fifteen packets on him only to realise his jacket was soaked through and so was the chisel!!! Sitting there for nearly two hours, we counted three buses going in the opposite direction. Turns out we were sitting on the wrong fucking side of the street. 3o'clock in the morning Rodders decided to ring his mum Pat, to pick us up she was fucking fuming, give Pat her due she came and picked us up love her. As the years went on I had two kids, Patsy and harry, which slowed me down so I didn't go out as much but Rodders went from strength to strength going out for four or five days at a time. I didn't realise how bad he actually was with the boozing and sniffing. We had a very good friend of ours called Vincent who died from cocaine poisoning. You would of thought that would of slowed Rod down but it didn't. I've gotta say I've never seen anyone drink and sniff the amount Rodders did but I must say the boy has done fucking fantastic. Really proud of him and proud to call him my mate. That's my story finished so I'm going down the pub!!!

Jim Grogan

September 1988

I first met Rodney when I started secondary school. We became friends through our love for football and video games. We played in the school football team together. Around this time is when we all met: Beddows, Gary, Ronnie, Jason, John, Burak and Curtis. We had a great time at school, we all should've knuckled down a bit more but we had a ball really. We used to hang about at lovel youth club on certain week days. The highlight was playing five-a-side in the hall with all the birds watching us!! When we were growing up we all had the same games consoles and used to swap games etc. Everyone used to pile round my house. Blinding days. I particularly remember a game called street fighter 2 which Rod's dad, Les bought him for Christmas for a small fortune which made him the envy of the gamers.

1994

This is when we all started going to the Moon and Sixpence on a Friday night. It was the highlight of the week. My mum used to give me £10, for that I would have four pints of stella and enough for a 'shit in a slipper' (kebab) on the way home! Rodney was the first out of our mob to have a mobile phone. I recall him getting it from Radio Rentals,up welling even when it was cut off. We used to make it ring on the bus and pretend to answer so we would look cool!! It was around this time when Rod used to play for Greenwich Borough. His mum Pat would pick me up in her white Nissan Micra and we would go and watch him play. I genuinely believe that if he learnt to control his temper while playing and got a lucky break he would've made it to a professional footballer. He was mustard.

Zen's nightclub

We used to go 'Uncle Ben's' on a Thursday night thinking we was the bollocks with our Ralph shirts on and copious amount of Joop fragrance. It was always a great night. Back then we never needed drugs to have a blinder. I often used to wake up at Rods house on a Friday morning feeling worse for wear! There was the odd tear-up with others but just fisticuffs, nothing major. Danny Dove and his brother Ben used to drive so we never had grief getting anywhere. One of the best nights ever was when the boxer, Nigel Benn was DJing. It was electric. So Thursday nights was Zenz and Moons was a Friday. Saturdays was Millwall and chill out with a joint and match of the day. We had a couple of places where we used to go in the cars to meet up and have a smoke,. One in Dartford and one up Shooters Hill. One particular night it was about 2am, we were in the car having a puff, all of a sudden some bloke walked past the car with an axe!!! You can imagine what that felt like when you are stoned. Next minute about fifteen of them went past with swords and shields., fuck that, let's get out of here. Turns out the soppy cunts were playing some role-play shit in the woods in the middle of the night!! My arsehole went I can tell you!!

Summer 1996

This without a doubt, was the best summers of our lives. We used to drink in the 'crook log' pub. There was about ten to fifteen of us as well as an older bunch of fellas. Euro '96 was on at the time. After the Spain game there was a punch up, the Old Bill turned up and someone got run over outside by a meat wagon. The police then escorted us all up the road to the polo bar. That night Gary had a party at his house it was a blinder. Someone put speed in Gary's mums drink and she was out of it!!!

John Cordier

Our friend John tragically took his own life in 2010. He was another that we all met at school. He was like my partner in crime. At school we were always getting into trouble together, bunking off to ride his motorbike over fanny on the hill. One time, Mrs Randall locked me and John in an empty class room for an hour as punishment. Imagine a teacher doing that these days. He was a Jack the lad type of bloke. His nickname was '40 large'. When we would go down the pub he would always pull out a big wad of dough to buy a drink!!! It was like he carried his wages about!! He had various old bangers we used to drive about in, "Rod Rod, Jim Jim, John John John in the metro all day long", was one of the silly songs we used to sing I miss him and wished we would've been closer as we got older. It makes you think that we all should make more effort to meet up. Life is far too short.

From a friends view by Natasha Philips

My first memories of Rodney are of him and his friend Steven Kempster up the Polobar in Bexleyheath. He was standing on a picnic table holding centre court in the middle of the outside terrace telling anyone that cared to listen about there recent holiday to Tenerif. Rod was saying that he had burnt his skin so badly that it was falling off in sheets, I think he was pulling his shirt up showing everyone, he was drinking a lot then but no more than any man that age. He was always known for fighting and getting into trouble but he was still liked and people thought he was funny. (a lovable rouge) this would be summer 1999 I then remember going up the Rat and Parrot Bexleyheath with my friends, Rod and his friend Scott was up there, we were having a quick drink before going clubbing up the Emporium Scott fancied coming but Rod didn't he was more of a pub person around that time. In June 2000 I started going out with one of Rods oldest friends Gary, in fact mine and Gary's first date Rod came with us with a few friends we had a good laugh. Rodney was getting known for getting into more fights, people were starting to become wary of being in his company, knowing that the laughing and joking Rod could turn into someone that was angry at the flick of a switch. He was never fighting with his friends and he would always have everyone's back but he was starting to get banned from more pubs. Some time later Rod was having girlfriend problems he wasn't getting on with the girl that was pregnant with his baby so by the time Jack was born things had gone sour with the mum and her family. Rod was over the moon to be a dad but looking back he was far too young and not ready. It pains me to say it but he wasn't giving it his all to be a dad I guess the mum and her family sensed that and along with his reputation it didn't do him any favours. Rod carried on living the weeks to drink the weekend and when we were all due to go out to a friends wedding we were nervous to how he would be, he come with his mum and I remember him walking into Gary's mums flat and I remember him looking so smart as he said "bit of tate n lyle hey Tash" The next few years me and Gary would hear who Rod was knocking about with knowing there was a few wronguns the fighting was getting even worse. He got arrested for causing a one man riot up the Golden Lion in Bexleyheath which did make us laugh. We still saw Rod every now and then but heard his drinking was getting worse. He came to Garys 30th in June 2007 to the Railway in Blackheath and he looked awful he turned up absolutely slaughtered and incohearant, he stayed a while but was getting increasingly angry with the pub being so busy and before he started and trouble he walked out on his own anyway and after that it was clear he had a big problem. Rod joined Facebook and would be the funniest guy on there one minute then a nightmare the next insulting everybody and telling them all to fuck off, by now the cocaine use must have been really bad because he was so paranoid he would accuse people of all sorts. Week in week out he would be on benders the weekends getting longer and longer he was falling out with his mum his friends no one could cope with him. Gary tried talking to him but he wouldn't have any of it though, everyone was getting more and more concerned about his behaviour. I bumped into his mum and she said she was really worried she hadn't heard from him, I messaged his sister Nicky saying we wished things would get better for him. I'm not sure anyone could have done anything though he was always adamant he would do what he wanted. Gary would speak to him but wouldn't really know what to say so always ended up passing the phone to me, I would just listen but I felt so sorry for him, I tried to convince him to take his heart medication even if it meant drinking with it. A little while later and Rod had just come out of rehab I popped in with my friends and Gary, Rod was unrecognisable he said he was trying his hardest not to drink and was only having orange but sadly I guessed by the way he kept going to the bar that he had swapped that orange for vodka, the temptation was too much he wasn't ready to be in that environment. Fasting forward to when we got the phone call to say he had cirrhosis of the liver and was bleeding everywhere Gary took the call and we both cried. He had been in rehab many times before and phoned us saying it was a waste of time and everybody was nuts but this time was different. We were terrified and he sounded scared. We wondered if it was too late had too much damage been done? I am happy to say that Rod is in such a better place I still have to take a second glance when I see him being so much more positive on social media and real life. Me and Gary could not be more happier and prouder of what he has done especially now helping others. The Rod we once knew is back and we coudn't be more prouder watching him marrying Leanne.

Dangers of mixing alcohol with cocaine - DICING WITH DEATH

If you are drinking alcohol and taking cocaine at the same time you really are dicing with death. Research has revealed a potentially dangerous interaction between cocaine and alcohol when taken together. The two drugs are converted by the body into a third drug called cocaethylene which affects the brain for longer and is more toxic than either drug alone. It heightens and intensifies the euphoric effect of cocaine, but also amplifies the depressive effect of alcohol. So you might feel on top of the world at the start of the night but as the evening wears on things get progressively worse. It puts an added strain on the body and the side effects include increased aggressive behaviour or getting into vulnerable situations. Cocaethylene also takes twice as long to be processed by the body than normal alcohol, and raises the risk to the liver and other parts of the body. There really is no answer to 'when the worst may happen it may be your first time or your 100th time, is it worth taking the chance'?? Medical and substance misuse professionals can only offer the quite firm recommendation of not to mix the two as there is no other harm minimization advice. The worst thing is you could be double dosing or actually forming cocaethylene if you have used cocaine the night before and been out drinking. Even if you have considered the consequences and decided to use and not drink cocaine is detectable in your body for three to five days and therefore if you have used on Friday night and then gone out for a drink on Saturday night you would still be introducing cocaethylene to your system. This works the same if you had a heavy drinking session and not allowed all the alcohol to have left your system before using cocaine. It's not quite as easy as not using the two on the same night. There is no simple equation that can be applied to work out the best time to mix them.

Facts about liver cirrhosis

Cirrhosis occurs when the liver has been inflamed for a long time, leading to scarring and a loss of function. This can be a life threatening condition. Cirrhosis damage is irreversible, but the patient can prevent further damage by avoiding alcohol. A long period of abstention can improve liver function, but if damage is permanent and severe, the patient may need a liver transplant to survive. During the early stage of cirrhosis the patient will feel tired and weak, their palms may be red and blotchy, they lose more weight, have itchy skin, insomnia, abdominal pain and tenderness plus also a loss of appetite. In end stage cirrhosis there will be hair loss and continued weight loss, jaundice, dark urine, black or pale stools, dizziness, fatigue, loss of libido, bleeding gums and nose, easily bruised skin, edema, vomiting, (with blood in the vomit) muscle cramps, irregular breathing, accelerated heartbeat, increased abdominal girth, personality changes, confusion, infections and walking problems for example staggering.

As the liver no longer processes toxins properly there will be heightened sensitivity to medications and alcohol.

After the brain, the liver is the most complex organ in the human body with over 500 functions. These include:

- Making proteins to fight infection and disease
- Filtering out blood toxins
- Manufacturing hormones, proteins and vital chemicals
- Regulating blood cholesterol and sugar levels
- Producing proteins that enable clotting and stop bleed following an injury

I would like to say thank you to my cardiologist, my gastrologist and my diabetic nurse for helping me lead a healthier, normal life. A special thank you to all my family and friends who contributed to my book, to Chris Hill who has been an amazing inspiration and to my beautiful wife, Leanne who without her none of this would be possible and without her I probably wouldn't be here today!

Lightning Source UK Ltd.
Milton Keynes UK
UKHW01f1807280918
329684UK00001B/144/P